Lutheran Identity

Other books in the Lutheran Voices series

Lutheran Identity

A Classical Understanding

Frank C. Senn

Augsburg Fortress

Minneapolis

To my colleagues in The Society of the Holy Trinity,
a pastoral oratory and ministerium,
who are renewing a sense of Lutheran identity
for the sake of the vows they took in ordination
to the Holy Ministry of Word and Sacrament.

LUTHERAN IDENTITY
A Classical Understanding

Purchases of ten or more copies of this book are available at a discount from the publisher. For more information, contact the sales department at Augsburg Fortress, Publishers, 1-800-328-4648, or write to: Sales Director, Augsburg Fortress, Publishers, Box 1209, Minneapolis, MN 55440-1209.

Cover photo © Stockbyte / Getty Images. Used by permission.

Library of Congress Cataloging-in-Publication Data
Senn, Frank C.
  Lutheran identity : a classical understanding / Frank C. Senn.
    p. cm.
  Includes bibliographical references.
  ISBN 978-0-8066-8010-1 (alk. paper)
  1. Lutheran Church—History. 2. Lutheran Church—Doctrines—History. I.Title.
BX8018.S46 2008
284.1—dc22   2007050843

The paper used in this publication meets the minimum requirements of American National Standard for Information Sciences—Permanence of Paper for Printed Library Materials, ANSI Z329.48-1984.
Manufactured in the U.S.A.

12   11   10   09   08   2   3   4   5   6   7   8   9   10

Contents

Preface

What does it mean to be a Lutheran? Recent discussion of Lutheran identity seems to be reduced to a few theological slogans, such as "justification by grace" (it should actually be "justification by faith"), "saint and sinner at the same time," "the priesthood of believers," and "theology of the cross" as opposed to a "theology of glory;" to which we could add "faith alone" (*sola fide*), "grace alone" (*sola gratia*), "Scripture alone" (*sola Scriptura*), "Christ alone" (*solus Christus*), and now "Word alone" (*solo Verbo*). Lutherans have enough theological solas to make up a whole choir! But real flesh-and-blood Lutheranism surely can't be reduced to a bunch of theological slogans.

Lutherans are heirs of a theological tradition and an ecclesiastical culture. We cannot avoid being identified with the Reformation that bears Luther's name, swept central and northern Europe in the sixteenth century, and became embedded in the folk cultures of those lands. We also participate in a tradition that is committed to the received canon of Holy Scripture, the ecumenical creeds, the Lutheran Confessions in *The Book of Concord*, the historic liturgical orders of Western Christianity, and practices of piety and public ministry.

I have written this little book especially for lay people (although clergy may find it helpful too). It seeks to explore, within the space allowed in this series, a classical understanding of Lutheranism. That means we will give more attention to earlier centuries than to our own. Lutheran tradition and culture are something to build on as we confront the possibilities and challenges of preaching, teaching, professing, and living the gospel of Jesus Christ in our own time and place. But we cannot abandon this tradition and step away from this culture without becoming something other than Lutheran. I hope to show that "Lutheran" is a good thing to be if that identification also includes openness to the whole (that is, the catholic) tradition.

Readers will notice that I make reference to both the Tappert and the Kolb/Wengert editions of *The Book of Concord*. I have no preference for one or the other. Which one I used depended on which one I could grab as I wrote these chapters. Both editions should be available in church libraries.

Some of the material in this book originated for a course I taught in the Hartwick Seminary Institute of Theology in the summer of 2006 on the campus of Hartwick College, Oneonta, New York. I developed it further as I was recovering from colon cancer surgery and undergoing chemotherapy. My thanks to Susan Johnson for intercepting the original manuscript and asking if I would be willing to publish in this series of "Lutheran Voices." Yes, I am; it's a good series. And I'm grateful to be a living Lutheran voice. Deo gratias.

Frank C. Senn
Evanston, Illinois

Advent 2007

1

From Reform Movement to Evangelical Catholic Church

I wouldn't be writing a book on "Lutheran identity" if it weren't for the sad state of divided Christianity. I would be writing about "Christian identity." But for five centuries, Lutherans have had to define themselves over against other Christian traditions—especially Roman Catholic on one side and the Reformed (that is, Calvinists) on the other. Because we will be contending that Lutheranism constitutes a true catholic faith, we should state upfront that Roman Catholicism, as we know it, is as much a product of the Reformation (by way of the reactions and renewal brought about by the Council of Trent) as Lutheranism, even though, like Lutheranism, it is in continuity with the Catholic Church before the Reformation. When I refer to the Catholic Church before the Reformation or catholic tradition generally, I do not mean Roman Catholic. The Reformed share many of the same Reformation teachings as Lutherans, such as justification by faith and the sole mediation of Christ between God and humanity, but differ from Lutheranism on the presence of Christ in Holy Communion and on the relationship of the Bible to church practice.

The schism in the sixteenth century that separated Lutherans, Roman Catholics, the Reformed, and others was not the first great schism in Christian history. The history of Christianity has been the story of conflict and division from the beginning. Already in the New Testament, we see instances of schism, specifically in the First Letter of John. Those who "have gone out from us" (1 John 2:19) are accused of lacking love, and "God is love" (4:18).

Church history includes dozens of little schisms but three major schisms. The first, in the fifth century, separated the church within the Byzantine Roman Empire from the churches outside of the empire. Next, in the eleventh century, a schism separated the church of the Byzantine East (based in Constantinople) from the church of the Latin West (based in Rome). And the sixteenth-century schism separated the churches in communion with the bishop of Rome in southern Europe from Protestant churches that broke relations with the papacy in northern Europe. Lutheranism is a product of the great schism of the sixteenth-century Reformation.

While doctrinal disagreements played a role in these schisms, cultural issues also were involved. In the first major schism, the East Syrian and Coptic churches embraced, respectively, the heresies of Nestorianism and Monophysitism partly as a way of resisting Byzantine (Greek) cultural imperialism. In 1054 Patriarch Michael Cerularius of Constantinople and Cardinal Humbert of Rome had a notorious quarrel that led to the mutual excommunications of the bishops of Rome and Constantinople. Doctrinal disagreements and differences in church practice dating back to the eighth century contributed to the mutual excommunications, but in spite of continuing efforts at cooperation and reconciliation, the West found the customs of the East strange, and the Byzantines regarded the Westerners as crude, lawless, and bellicose. We will discuss some of the doctrinal and cultural issues that contributed to the sixteenth century schism in Western Christianity in the next section. But let us at least observe here that the Renaissance, which provides a cultural backdrop to the Reformation, focused more on the visual arts in southern Europe and more on literature in western Europe and that this has consequences on Roman Catholic and Protestant forms of devotion.

Luther's Reform Movement

Martin Luther's (1483–1546) life story can be read in many fine biographies, and I will not rehearse it here. What is important to note for Lutheran identity is that Luther came to religious certainty as a result of his studies and lectures on the Bible, especially the Psalms and

Paul's letters to the Romans and Galatians. Luther's insight that we cannot merit God's favor by our good works, that we must depend on God's justification of the sinner for the sake of his Son, Jesus Christ, whose death on the cross atoned for all sins once and for all, constituted a veritable Copernican revolution in theology. This insight led Luther to a critical assessment of many church practices, especially in the area of religious good works, that could only constitute in his eyes "works righteousness," the attempt to win God's favor by performing works rather than by trusting in God's promises. He added to Paul's quote from Habbakuk 2:4 in Romans 3:28, "a person is justified by faith" the word *alone.* Inspired by his work on Galatians, considered the testament of Christian freedom, Martin Ludder changed his name to "Luther," from the Greek *elutherius*, "freedom."

From 1517 on, Luther also began to write pamphlets calling for reform. Luther's reform proposals did not constitute the first movement calling for reform in the Catholic Church of the West. In fact, Heiko Oberman writes that Reformation was really "a medieval event."[1] The medieval monasteries in particular were always going through reforms to return to the original letter and spirit of their "Rules," which some-times produced new monastic orders or observant branches of existing orders. Luther belonged to the Observant Branch of the Hermits of Saint Augustine; he had become a part of the reform leadership even in the observant branch. By the late Middle Ages, even as late as 1517, there were also movements for reform through general councils, but little came of these efforts.

Luther's Reformation was also "a German event."[2] There was a long history of tension between Holy Roman Emperors (who were de facto kings of Germany) and the papacy in Rome. Grievances against Rome seem to have been greater in Germany than in other countries in Europe. Luther struck a chord of German nationalism with his calls for reform. When a papal bull proclaimed his excommunication in 1520 and an imperial decree made him an outlaw in 1521, he was protected by his powerful prince, Frederick the Wise, elector of Saxony, and Frederick's successor, John the Steadfast. In fact, the young Emperor Charles V found it difficult to proceed against Luther because he could not afford to alienate the princes who espoused Luther's teaching, since he needed their military support in his campaign against the Muslim Turks, who were advancing up the Danube River to the very gates of the traditional Hapsburg seat of Vienna. In a certain sense, the Muslims gave Lutheranism cover to develop freely in Germany without being squashed by his Catholic Majesty, Charles V, who might have used his Spanish troops to do the job.[3]

As social and cultural as well as theological issues were involved in previous schisms, this was also the case in Luther's Reformation. His Reformation is said to have been inaugurated on October 31, 1517, the eve of All Saints' Day, when Professor Luther of the University of Wittenberg posted on the door of the Castle Church his Ninety-Five Theses concerning the sale of indulgences, intending to debate the issue. Lutherans today can hardly understand what the issue was all about because we have no experience of indulgences. Originally, they were a form of penance conveying pardon for sin after undertaking a religious work such as a pilgrimage or making a financial contribution. The particular indulgence sold by the Dominican Johann Tetzel granted full forgiveness of all sins that could be applied even to souls in purgatory. Luther the pastor experienced how these indulgences were undermining the sacrament of penance among his parishioners. He did not realize that these indulgences were promulgated by a special deal arranged between Pope Leo X and Albrecht of Brandenburg. Under that arrangement, Albrecht became archbishop of both Magdeburg and Mainz, in return for which he allowed a special plenary indulgence to be sold in his territories, the proceeds of which would go to the construction of the new Saint Peter's Basilica in Rome.

Luther intended his theses for academic debate. His theological position was transparent in his theses when he wrote:

When our Lord and Master Jesus Christ said, "repent," [Matt. 4:17] he willed the entire life of believers to be one of repentance. . . .

Any truly repentant Christian has a right to full remission of penalty and guilt, even without indulgence letters.

Any true Christian, whether living or dead, participates in all the blessings of Christ and the church, and this is granted him by God, even without indulgence letters.[4]

But then Luther went on to charge that the revenues of all Christendom were being sucked into this insatiable basilica, that the pope would do better to sell Saint Peter's and give the money to the poor, that the pope cannot remove or reduce the penalties of purgatory, because these have been imposed by God, that the saints have no extra credits to give to sinners, and that the pope has no jurisdiction over purgatory, but if he does, he should, out of Christian love, release all the souls in purgatory.

Two things Luther did in his theses earned him the wrath of papal supporters and traditional religionists: he challenged the authority of the pope, and he called into question the whole seamless community between the living and the dead that existed in medieval Christianity. His challenge of papal authority was brought out by Johann Eck in a great debate that was arranged in Leipzig in 1519. Although the debate was supposed to be on the matter of indulgences (in response to Luther's Ninety-Five Theses), Eck managed to make the whole discussion turn on the issue of papal authority: Luther's thesis that the pope cannot remit penalties in purgatory. In the give-and-take of the debate, Eck forced Luther to admit that popes and councils could err, and when asked what he would put in their place, Luther answered: the authority of Scripture alone. He did not answer the question of teaching authority in the church other than to say, "A simple lay person armed with Scripture is to be believed above a pope or council without it."[5] One can imagine the revolutionary impact of such a statement when it was reported to the general public.

In the matter of the seamless community between the living and the dead, social historian Edward Muir writes, "The Reformation, particularly in its early phases, can be seen as a forceful rejection of the ritual industry of death with all its expensive commitments to priestly intervention."[6] This expensive priestly intervention included anniversary masses, votive masses for the repose of souls in purgatory, and chantries that sang prayer offices of the dead for departed bene-factors of monasteries and churches in perpetuity—all of which were paid for by the living as a form of charity to the dead, whose souls were presumed to be in purgatory, being purified to enter heaven. One after another, the Reformers began to question even the existence of purga-tory. Luther himself finally wrote a tract in 1530 entitled *Rejection of Purgatory*. In the Smalcald Articles of 1537, he held that purgatory is "contrary to the fundamental article that Christ alone, and not the work of man, can help souls. Besides, nothing has been commanded or enjoined upon us [in Scripture] with reference to the dead."[7] Cutting the interaction between the living and the dead constituted a major cultural change as well as a doctrinal change since so much of the social and religious apparatus of the Middle Ages presumed a communion between this life and the afterlife.

Luther had already struck at masses being offered for the living as well as the dead. In the second of his three reformatory treatises of 1520, *The Babylonian Captivity of the Church*, Luther took up the whole sacramental system of the medieval church with its seven sacraments and held that there were only three instituted by Christ: baptism, the Eucharist, and penance or the office of the keys. Confirmation, ordina-tion, marriage, and anointing of the sick and dying were rites developed by the church for its own pastoral needs, not sacraments commanded by Christ. Luther charged that the papists were holding the Sacrament of the Altar (also called Holy Communion, the Lord's Supper, or the Eucharist) captive by three walls. The first wall was withholding the cup from lay communicants. The second was teaching the doctrine of transubstantiation (that the substance of the bread and wine are changed into the body and blood of Christ by virtue of the words of Christ, while the accidents of bread and wine remain unchanged), which he regarded as a scholastic attempt to explain what should remain a mystery of faith. The third wall was offering the Mass as a good work and sacrifice that we present to God, rather than receiving the gift of communion as Christ's last will and testament to his people. The terms *good work* and *sacrifice* suggest two different papist errors: the Mass cannot be a good work that we offer to God when it is a gift Christ offers to us, and the Mass cannot be a sacrifice offered for special intentions when it should be a proclamation and reception of the benefits of Christ's atoning sacrifice, especially the forgiveness of sins. This attack on the Mass as a sacrifice struck down votive masses, which were masses offered for special intentions, including the relief of souls in purgatory. It should be understood that the sacrifice of the Mass had been an integral part of a whole religious and cultural system that provided an identity to Christian peoples. It was not just the issue of monetary transactions but the whole relationship between the living and the dead that Luther struck down with his rejection of the sacrifice of the Mass.

Luther's first reformatory treatise, *An Open Letter to the Christian Nobility of the German Nation Concerning the Reform of the Christian Estate* (1520), was equally radical but based on tradition. This detailed analysis of the deformation of the society of Christendom was actually a response to a request for such an analysis from officials in the Saxon court and other influential Germans. Praising the newly elected Emperor Charles V as a divine sign of a "time of grace," Luther called for the demolition of three walls behind which papal authority had been established: the notion that there is a divinely instituted spiritual difference between clergy and laity, the claim that only the pope can interpret Scripture, and the assertion that only the pope can call an ecumenical council and approve its decisions. Against these walls, Luther pointed out that all Christians have equal status before God on the basis of their baptism, that anyone may interpret the Bible, and that the great ecumenical councils of the ancient church were convened by the emperor. He called on Emperor Charles V to convene an ecumenical council to deal with the abuses in doctrine and practice in the Catholic Church and called on the German nobility to assume responsibility for the church as the principal lay leaders. They would become, in effect, "emergency bishops" because the pope and the bishops had betrayed the gospel and would not reform the church. Thus, Luther appealed to the tradition of Roman emperors convening councils of the church and princes and rulers exercising episcopal functions within their territories. This argument was not lost on rulers, even those outside the

Holy Roman Empire, such as Henry VIII in England and Gustav I Vasa in Sweden.

Emergence of Evangelical Catholic Churches

In Saxony, the elector took a hands-off policy with regard to reform, even though he couldn't personally follow Luther into an Evangelical Church. After Luther's trial for heresy at the Diet (imperial parliament) of Worms, Frederick secretly arranged for Luther to be "incarcerated" as a guest in the Wartburg Castle for safekeeping. While in Wartburg in 1521–1522, Luther wrote tracts and engaged in the translation of the New Testament into idiomatic German.

In the meantime, Andreas Bodenstein von Karlstadt, dean of the theology faculty, led the Wittenbergers on an iconoclastic binge, destroying statues, paintings, stained glass, altars, candlesticks, and crucifixes that he thought got in the way of the believer's relationship with God. The ensuing social chaos prompted Luther to return to Wittenberg to take control of his own reformation. The theology faculty, at Luther's urging, asked Carlstadt to leave town, and Luther preached eight sermons in eight days to restore order. The experience of this iconoclasm led Luther to adopt a go-slow approach, especially in matters concerning worship. Nevertheless, the New Testament began to be read in German in the churches, private and votive masses were abolished, Luther developed congregational forms of matins and vespers (morning and evening prayer) to replace the weekday masses, and he prepared forms for the celebration of the Mass in Latin and in German.

In 1525 Elector Frederick and Crown Prince John met with leading members of the Saxon clergy to create the Wittenberg Church Order to regulate church teaching and practice throughout Electoral Saxony. The rulers proclaimed the first duty of the clergy to be preaching the gospel "pure, clean, and clear, without any admixture of human doctrines." By 1527 it was considered time to undertake a visitation of all the parishes in Electoral Saxony to see how the course of reformation was going. Because the bishops were not visiting as they should, Luther and his young humanist colleague, Philipp Melanchthon, prepared *Articles of Visitation* for a visitation of the parishes in Saxony that took place in 1528 under the authority of the new elector, John the Steadfast, who embraced Luther's Reformation. The experience of the dismal state of spiritual life of the parishes induced Luther in 1529 to prepare his *Small Catechism* for use in the homes of Christians and a *Large Catechism* for the instruction of pastors and teachers.

The Reformation was adopted in the cities and lands of the Holy Roman Empire by a deliberate decision of the authorities, whether city councils or princes. The first city to adopt Luther's reformation was the free imperial city of Nuremberg. A pattern was followed here that was also played out in other free cities. A Reformer was called as preacher of the great church of the city. The controversies following from the preaching for reform led to public debates between Reformers and traditionalists. The city council decided which side had won the debate and acted to implement reforms. This is the way the Reformation was officially legalized in other cities such as Ulm, Zurich, Basel, Geneva, Strassburg, and even Regensberg (which opted for a Catholic reform). The Swedish capital of Stockholm adopted the Lutheran Reformation after a similar process in 1530, even though this was without the full commitment of the king and was not immediately embraced by the rest of the country.

For centuries the German rulers had been virtual bishops over their own realms. They controlled or influenced much of the public religious life, from the appointment of clergy to prominent positions to the sale of indulgences (from which they took a cut). In a sense, Elector John of Saxony, Duke John Frederick of Saxony, Landgrave Philip of Hesse, Margrave Casimir of Brandenburg and his successor, Elector George of Brandenburg, Duke Christian of Schleswig-Holstein, and Duchess Elizabeth of Brunswick-Lüneberg were following tradition when they took steps to implement the Lutheran Reformation in their realms and consulted with the Reformers in the drafting and promulgation of church orders to regulate faith and practice. When a statement of Lutheran faith and practice, later called the Augsburg Confession, was presented to Emperor Charles V at the Diet of Augsburg on June 25, 1530, it was signed by some of the territorial princes and mayors of the free cities and received by others as the basis for reforming faith and practice.

The spread of the Reformation to the Scandinavian countries was a slower process. Reformation ideas reached Scandinavian and Baltic port cities including Copenhagen, Bergen, Stockholm, Riga, and Turku through the German merchants of the Hanseatic League. But except for Denmark, these countries were large and had conservative populations. Gustav I Vasa had come to the throne of Sweden in 1523 after a war of independence from Denmark. He appreciated the preaching of Reformers like Olavus Petri and recognized the advantage of appropriating the wealth of the monasteries, the bishoprics, and even the poor parishes for his impoverished treasury.[8] But no fewer than five rebellions broke out against the king's church policy during King Gustav I's reign. Since he was an elected monarch, he felt deeply the need for legitimacy that could be conferred through a coronation at which recognized bishops officiated. For the coronation of his queen in 1531, he desired a properly consecrated and installed archbishop of Uppsala (the primatial or first-established seat of the church in Sweden). Two archbishops recognized by Rome were already contending for the see, but both were absent from the country, so Gustav set aside the rights of the cathedral chapter and convened a synod of clergy from throughout Sweden to elect a new archbishop. They chose Laurentius, the thirty-two-year-old younger brother of Olavus Petri, who, like his brother, had studied at Wittenberg. The king prevailed on the existing bishops to consecrate Laurentius, with or without papal approval. As a result, the apostolic succession of bishops was retained in Sweden and was extended to the Duchy of Finland, which was under Swedish administration. Nevertheless, it took until 1571 for Sweden to have an official church order to regulate faith and practice throughout the whole realm. The Augsburg Confession was not received until 1593, when the country faced a constitutional crisis because the heir apparent, Sigismund III, was also the king of Poland and a zealous promoter of the Counter-Reformation.

In Denmark, the Reformation was implemented in almost one fell swoop when the Lutheran Duke Christian of Schleswig-Holstein became King Christian III of Denmark, Norway, and Iceland. In 1537 the new king borrowed from the elector of Saxony Pastor Johannes Bugenhagen, who had already consulted on and helped draft half a dozen church orders in northern Germany, to prepare a Danish church order. Bugenhagen also officiated at the coronation of the king and queen. King Christian thereupon deposed the seven Catholic bishops in Denmark and Norway and had seven evangelical superintendents installed in their place, with Bugenhagen officiating at their consecrations. Reformation faith and practice spread quickly in Denmark but more slowly throughout Norway and Iceland because there were no prominent Reformers in these countries, the people were religiously conservative, there was no supply of evangelical pastors to put in place of the priests who had been serving parishes in these countries, and it took time to translate the liturgy and the Bible into these Scandinavian languages.

The Reformation spread to the Baltic countries through German merchants of the Hanseatic League and the Teutonic knights. The country of Livonia comprised both Latvia and Estonia. As in Scandinavia, reform began first in the towns (Riga, Revel, and Dorpat) in the 1520s and spread slowly to the countryside. A part of the social and cultural dynamic here was that the Germans in the towns had Reformation resources in their own language; it took time to translate the Bible, liturgy, and catechism into the Estonian and Latvian languages.[9]

Lutheran Denominations

The Christian religion in Europe was either an established, state-supported church or a sect that existed on the margins of church and society (for example, as Anabaptists and pietistic groups). For most of its history, Lutheranism in Europe was the established church of the city or land and was tied in with the state as a tax-supported institution. The idea of a state-supported church is foreign to Christians living in the United States, where the Constitution prohibits establishing one particular church or sect as a national religion. Lutherans in North America live in religiously pluralistic societies in which Christianity is broken up into hundreds of denominations, including several Lutheran denominations. From the beginning, American denominations embodied aspects of both a church and a sect in that they were comprehensive of their share of the population but needed to maintain discipline in faith and practice in order to set themselves off from other denominations. In other words, everyone is welcome to join, but to remain a member in good standing, one must show a commitment to the particular beliefs and practices of this denomination and this congregation by regularly participating in worship and by financially supporting this church's ministries.

In 1742, when Henry Melchior Muhlenberg was sent from Halle, Germany, to be pastor of the Lutherans in Pennsylvania, his idea was to "plant the Church." To this end, he organized in 1748 a ministerium of the German-speaking pastors, no matter what their land of origin. His idea was to draw Lutheran settlers into one church body with one worship book. Various synods were organized in the eastern states in the early nineteenth century, and these were eventually joined into the General Synod of the Evangelical Lutheran Church. The United Synod of the South separated from the General Synod during the Civil War, and the General Council was formed because of doctrinal disagreements within the General Synod. However, in 1918, these three federations of synods were finally brought into the United Lutheran Church in America (ULCA). A further merger of the ULCA with the Swedish Augustana, Danish, and Finnish synods created the Lutheran Church in America in 1962. As immigrants came from various countries in Europe throughout the nineteenth century, they set up ethnic synods based on language use. Several midwestern German synods merged in 1930 to form the American Lutheran Church, and then merged with Danish and Norwegian churches to form a new American Lutheran Church in 1960. The Lutheran Church in America and the American Lutheran Church then merged in 1987, along with the Association of Evangelical Lutheran Churches, a secessionist group from The Lutheran Church–Missouri Synod, to form the Evangelical Lutheran Church in America.

The story of the Missouri Synod is different. It was founded in 1847 by settlers from Saxony who had settled in the Mississippi and

Missouri Valleys to escape being forced into a union of Lutherans and Reformed in Germany. After a troubling episode with their first leader, Bishop Martin Stefan, Pastor C. F. W. Walther succeeded in rallying the congregations and pastors into a synod. This synod has exemplified throughout its history more of the sectarian than the churchly aspects of American denominations in the sense of maintaining discipline in their distinctive beliefs and practices. Nevertheless, the Missouri Synod has not been able to avoid the comprehensive character of American denominations, especially in recent years as it has embraced the principles of church growth coming out of American evangelicalism.

The Marks of the Church

Whether it is a European state church or an American-type denomination, how can a Lutheran church be an evangelical catholic church? "Evangelical" implies an emphasis on God's saving acts in Jesus Christ. "Catholicity" implies continuity with the church universal in both historical length and global breadth. The question of whether there could be a true catholic church apart from the historical continuity of bishops and the universal episcopate of the bishop of Rome (the pope) was put to Luther even before there were evangelical churches. He answered his papist critics in his 1520 treatise *On the Papacy at Rome* by developing "marks of the church" (*notae ecclesiae*). In this treatise, he distinguished between the social and political reality of the church as a community in fellowship with the Roman see and the true church seen as "a community or assembly of the saints in faith." He went on to say, "Not Rome or this place or that place, but baptism, the sacrament, and the gospel are the signs by which the existence of the Church in the world can be noticed externally."[10]

Luther continued to teach that the true church can be seen where the gospel is preached and the sacraments of Christ are administered. Any church that has the gospel and the sacraments is a true church, even if some aspects of its teaching are in error and its practices questionable—including, in Luther's view, the Church of Rome. Philipp Melanchthon used this teaching as the basis for church unity in article 7 of the Augsburg Confession:

It is also taught that at all times there must be and remain one holy, Christian church. It is the assembly of all believers among whom the gospel is purely preached and the holy sacraments are administered according to the gospel.

For this is enough for the true unity of the Christian church that there the gospel is preached harmoniously according to a pure understanding and the sacraments are administered in conformity with the divine Word. It is not necessary for the true unity of the Christian church that uniform ceremonies, instituted by human beings, be observed everywhere. As Paul says in Ephesians 4 [verses 4-5]: "There is one body and one Spirit, just as you were called to the one hope of your calling, one Lord, one faith, one baptism."[11]

Again, in a long section in his treatise *On Councils and the Church* (1539), written in despair that a free general council would ever be called to deal with theological differences and practical abuses, Luther reiterated the marks of the church in a longer list:[12]

1. The public preaching of the Word of God, rightly distinguishing law and gospel
2. The sacrament of baptism
3. The sacrament of the altar
4. The office of the keys (Matthew 18), publicly exercised
5. The ordination or calling of ministers
6. Prayer, public praise, and thanksgiving to God
7. The possession of the holy cross in the suffering of the saints

In addition, Luther went on to say Christians would be identified externally by signs of the sanctifying work of the Holy Spirit in their lives as they observed the second table of Moses, that is, the commandments having to do with honoring parents and others in authority and serving neighbors.

Thus, the evangelical catholicity of Lutheranism is demonstrated by outward marks that are catholic (whole tradition) in form but evangelical (gospel centered) in content. Where evidence of these practices exists, there is a true catholic church, ostensibly in fellowship with every other church in which these "marks" are evident. Word and sacrament are enough (*satis est*) for Christian unity. Unfortunately, other matters tend to keep Christians divided, and in the situation of denomination-alism, competition between denominations (even Lutheran denomi-nations) is inevitable for institutional perpetuation and survival. Our concern in this little book is to open up the elements that constitute a true Lutheran identity. Without insisting on a false uniformity, Christians should seek unity in these marks of the true church.

Questions for Discussion

1. Lutheran theologian Jaroslav Pelikan called the Reformation a "tragic necessity." On the basis of this chapter, why was it tragic? Why was it necessary?

2. In what ways did the adoption of the Reformation maintain con-tinuity with the pre-Reformation church in the cities and lands of Europe? In what ways did it represent discontinuity?

3. How does the American system of denominationalism contribute to or hinder Christian unity?

4. Where do you see the outward marks of the churches in congrega-tions and larger church bodies today?

2

The Canon of Scripture

The chief book of the Reformation was the Bible. Martin Luther's personal struggle to find a gracious God was accompanied by a search of the Scriptures. His doctorate was in the Bible, and he was a biblical exegete above everything else. His call for the reform of church and society was based on the gospel that he found in the Bible. Luther and the other Reformers set the authority of Scripture over against all other authorities, if they disagreed with each other. This is what *sola Scriptura* is all about: the authority of Scripture as "the only rule and norm according to which all doctrines and teachers alike must be appraised and judged."[1]

What it means to call Scripture "rule and norm" needs to be clearly understood. For the Reformed churches, Scripture is the "source" of church teaching and practice. This sometimes got them into difficulty over teachings and practices that are not clearly defined in the Bible, such as the doctrine of the Trinity or the practice of infant baptism. For Lutherans, church doctrine and practice need not be found in the Bible, but they must not be in conflict with the clear word of Scripture.

Luther's greatest contribution to German culture was probably his translation of the Bible into German from the original languages of Hebrew and Greek. However, we should not think the Bible was unavailable before Luther came along. Admittedly, it was not available in mass quantities, because hand-produced manuscripts were expensive. The mass reproduction of Bibles was made possible by Gutenberg's invention of movable type in the late fifteenth century. This information revolution was providential in that it occurred just on the eve of the Reformation, and the Reformers made great use of this new technology. We should also note that there had been translations of the Bible into vernacular languages before Luther. Even the Latin Vulgate was a translation—the work of Jerome in the fourth century—and it was as significant a contribution to medieval Latin culture as Luther's German Bible was to modern German culture. But the success of Luther's translation spurred worthy translations into other languages, including English, French, and Swedish.

The Bible in Lutheran use is not opposed to the Catholic tradition; it is a gift of the Catholic tradition. I say this because the canon of Scripture was assumed in Lutheranism. There is no place in the Lutheran Confessions where a canon or list of biblical books is given. In contrast, the Reformed Confessions spell out the canon: the sixty-six books of the Old and New Testaments. Authorized English versions of the Bible, such as the King James Version of 1611, were produced by scholars in the Reformed tradition, so they include those sixty-six books but not the Apocrypha, a set of books between the testaments (although the Apocrypha was translated separately and read as edifying literature). Like the Latin Vulgate, Luther's German Bible does include the Apocrypha, and apocryphal writings continued to be used liturgically in Lutheran worship. This distinction became an issue only because the Council of Trent, which Protestants did not attend, in reaction to the Reformed Confessions, included the Apocrypha in the category of "deutero-canonical" (secondary canonical) writings. But Lutheran liturgies have used some apocryphal material, including the Prayer of Manasseh as a prayer of confession, and the Song of the Three Young Men (*Benedicite opera omnia;* "All you works of the Lord") sometimes sung in matins.

The Christological Interpretation of the Bible

As far as Luther was concerned, what is important about the Bible is that it conveys Christ (*was Christum treibt*). Even within the recognized canon, Luther thought, some books convey the gospel of Christ better than other books (for example, Romans more than James). Indeed, Luther demonstrated a theological criticism of the Bible that was not replicated in post-Reformation Lutheran orthodoxy, with its doctrine of biblical inerrancy. Orthodox Lutheranism in the period after Luther used the Bible as proof texts to defend doctrines. The historical criticism of the Bible that began in the Age of Enlightenment, and has continued unabated for two centuries, assaulted the orthodox use of the Bible by placing every book and text in its historical and cultural context. Historical criticism has been helpful for understanding the historical and cultural context of biblical stories and texts but not helpful for receiving the Bible as the living word of God that conveys Christ. That use of the Bible is most evident in its liturgical use.

The canon of Scripture is indissolubly linked with the liturgical use of the Bible. The early Christian liturgical assemblies (*ecclesiae*) gathered to read what Justin Martyr called "the writings of the prophets" and "the memoirs of the apostles." This translates into what later Christians called the Old and New Testaments, which synods and councils in the East and the West canonized as one collection of sacred scripture. The canonical Hebrew Scriptures were a given for Christians. The Christ-event made no sense apart from its Old Testament background. Indeed, the only interpretation of the Christ-event in the canonical gospels was that such-and-such happened "to fulfill what was written in the scriptures" or "to fulfill what was spoken by the prophet."

This is why, in the Christian Bible, the Old Testament books are arranged in collections of (1) historical books, (2) writings, and (3) prophets, in contrast to the Jewish *Tanakh*, in which the order is (1) historical books, (2) prophets, and (3) writings. In the Christian Bible, the last prophetic book, Malachi, leads directly to the first gospel, Matthew, which stresses prophecy fulfillment even more than the other gospels do. In Matthew 5:17-18, Jesus himself taught that he had not come to abolish the law but to fulfill it. This claim does not extend only to the moral law of the "second table" of the Ten Commandments, but it also includes the ceremonial law of the Pentateuch (the five Books of Moses). None of it will pass away until all that God has commanded in it is fulfilled by Christ's perfect obedience to the Father. He accomplished this by his incarnation, the sacrifice of his life, his atoning sacrifice, and his resurrection and ascension to the place of authority—that is, "at the right hand of the God the Father almighty," as we confess in the creed.

Some Lutherans have argued that the apostle Paul contradicts this by declaring that Christ is the end of the law (Rom. 10:4). In his flesh, he has "abolished the law of the commandments with its ritual decrees" (Eph. 2:15). Yet Paul himself maintains that he did not abolish the law by preaching faith in Christ; instead, he upheld the law (Rom. 3:31). This was because Christ had actually accomplished everything that the law required (Rom. 8:3-4). Christians, therefore, are freed from the law's condemnation. At the same time, by the sanctifying work of the Holy Spirit, they are led to live in harmony with the law, not in sinful violation of it (Rom. 6:1-14; 8:1-8; Gal. 3:13-14; 5:16-24). This is what Paul means by "the circumcision of Christ" in Col. 2:11; we have been discharged from the law's implacable demands and now serve God in the spirit of the law, in the Holy Spirit (Rom. 7:4, 6).

The Process of Canonization

The church made no decision about which Hebrew books were canonical. It accepted the decisions of the rabbis in terms of which writings were inspired. The one thing we have to be careful about is that the New Testament writers used the Greek translation of the Hebrew Scriptures, the Septuagint, so there is some discrepancy between quotations of the Old Testament in the New and the actual Old Testament texts in Hebrew. This sometimes has doctrinal significance, as when the Septuagint version of Isaiah 7:10 says, "A virgin shall conceive and bear a son," rather than, "A young woman shall conceive," as the Hebrew has it.

The gospels and letters of the apostles became canonical scripture because (1) an apostolic authority was believed to lie behind them and (2) they were read in the Christian liturgical assemblies along with the Hebrew Scriptures. The reading of scripture in the Christian assemblies made the Bible the church's book. The books that were read in the liturgical assembly constituted the canon; those that were not read were rejected from the canon. There were also gnostic gospels, which were eliminated from the canon because they did not convey Christ as being true man as well as true God, subject to suffering and death as well as resurrection and glory.

The earliest list of canonical books is from a fragment first published in 1740 by the Italian scholar Ludovico Muratori. It lists the books read in the Church of Rome in about A.D. 200. Interestingly, it does not include Hebrews, James, 2 and 3 John, 1 and 2 Peter, Jude, or the Revelation to Saint John the Seer. These books were the most disputed in terms of being included in the canon. The most disputed of all, in terms of whether it should be included in the canon, was Revelation. However, the writings of Eusebius of Caesarea and his contemporary Athanasius of Alexandria make it clear that the canon as we know it was coming to a definitive close by the middle of the fourth century. In 382, a synod held in Rome under Pope Damasus adopted, under the influence of Jerome, the list of books found in a pastoral letter of Bishop Athanasius, dated 367. The same list was confirmed independently for the Province of Africa in a synod held in Hippo Regius in 393, and again in Carthage in 397 and 419, under the leadership of Bishop Augustine of Hippo. Thus, by the beginning of the fifth century, the canon of Scripture was settled in the Western church, and this was ratified by Pope Gelasius at the end of the fifth century. The question of the canon was settled and closed for the Eastern Church by the Second Council of Trullo in 692 with the same list of New Testament books that had been approved in the Western Church.

The Bible in the Liturgy

Because those books were canonized that were read in the liturgical assembly, the liturgy is Scripture's home. More than this, however, the Bible is the historic liturgy's primary text. By historic liturgy, I mean the orders of public worship that actually developed in the ancient church and continued to evolve during the Middle Ages. It is not based on the Bible as if there were a prescribed order of worship in the New Testament, but in the sense that the text of the Bible pervades the historic liturgy. The texts of the Sacred Scriptures of the Old and New Testaments provide words for the liturgical assembly's praise of God, confession of sins, profession of faith, intercessions, thanksgiving, and supplication and also the meaning of the assembly's ritual actions and symbols.[2]

The heart of the Liturgy of the Word is the reading and exposition of Scripture. Orders of service currently in use follow several versions of the three-year lectionary cycle, a prescribed list of Bible readings for Sundays and festivals that was first developed in the Roman Lectionary of the Mass. The various lectionaries now in use—Roman, Revised Common Lectionary—provide for a first reading from the Old Testament or the book of Acts during Easter, psalmody sung in response to the first reading, a second reading from a New Testament epistle, and a gospel reading.

The gospel is considered the primary reading. Over the course of three years, the four gospels are read almost in their entirety: Matthew in Year A, Mark in Year B, Luke in Year C, and John in Year B and during the festival seasons of Christmas and Easter. Old Testament readings are chosen primarily for their typological relationship to the gospel (as described in the next section of this chapter). The second reading consists of pericopes, or selections from particular New Testament books, during the Advent-Christmas and Lent-Easter cycles but semi-continuous readings of whole epistles during the time after Epiphany and after Pentecost. Practically the entire New Testament and a substantial portion of the Old Testament are read over the course of three years.

Revised orders of Mass or the Service of Holy Communion place the homily or sermon immediately after the gospel reading. The purpose of the homily or sermon in the liturgy is to open up the Scriptures by explicating the texts in their biblical context and applying them to the contemporary context of the assembly. Luther regarded the oral preaching of the word of God as one of three meanings of the term *the word of God*. The other two are the Word made flesh in Jesus the Christ (the incarnation or "enfleshment" of the word) and the words of Scripture, which are vehicles of the word of God. All three understandings of *word of God* convey Christ—the incarnation, Scripture, and the sermon.

Typological Interpretation of the Bible

A primary principle of biblical interpretation for the Reformers was that Scripture interprets Scripture. This means that Scripture is clear in its message, and clearer passages can be used to shed light on more obscure passages. The liturgy relates to this principle in its use of typology. Typology means that one particular act is replicated in further acts. The theological value of this method is that it is the way in which God acts in the Bible.[3] For example, God acts to save Israel by bringing the Israelites through water and wilderness to the promised land, first through the crossing of the sea and then through the crossing of the River Jordan, in which Jesus was later baptized. The exodus becomes a type of the passover of Christ through death to new and glorified life in the resurrection. It also becomes a type of initiation that is replicated in Christian baptism. Or, again, God acts to make the youngest son of a shepherd family in the smallest tribe of Israel the anointed king of Israel (in fact, Israel's greatest king). So God's own anointed Servant-Son is born in humility in David's little town of Bethlehem and extends the kingdom of God through his obedience to the Father by means of weakness rather than self-assertion and strength.

Luther himself endorsed the typological interpretation of the Bible because it is a way of proclaiming Christ throughout the whole Bible. In his *Confession Concerning Christ's Supper*, he says, "God always works so that the figure or type appears first, and then the true reality and fulfillment of the type follows. So the Old Testament first comes forth as a type, and the New Testament follows as the true reality."[4] Thus, the Old Testament is read by the liturgical assembly neither as a historical record, nor as a foil against which the gospel stands, but as the root from which the gospel springs. As Luke reports, Jesus explains to the disciples on the road to Emmaus after his resurrection "all the things about himself in all the scriptures" (Luke 24:27).

The details of Christ's trial and execution found in the passion narratives rely as much, if not more, on the Psalms than on eyewitness accounts. In fact, if we ask what is the meaning of the Christ-event in the gospels, the only answer given by the evangelists is that "such-and-such took place to fulfill what was written by the prophets." Thus, the primary reason that Christians should know the Old Testament is that without such knowledge, their understanding of the New Testament will be limited, even erroneous. Christians need not be biblical scholars or students of ancient Near Eastern documents, but they need to encounter the New Testament and its proclamation of Jesus Christ, and to do that well, they need to know the story of Israel.

We need both Old and New Testaments in our liturgies. It was an important aspect of liturgical renewal in the late twentieth century that all the liturgical traditions recovered the Old Testament reading and the psalmody that gives us a response to the first reading. If we tie the Old Testament to the New, we demonstrate the reliance of the New on the Old. If, on the other hand, we proclaim the Old without reference to the New, the question about why Christians are reading those books at all remains unanswered. It is the task of preachers to show Christ in the Old Testament as well as in the New by employing the typological interpretation needed to tie together the readings in the lectionary. A typological and christological reading of the Old Testament can even help contemporary Christians deal with some of the Old Testament narratives, with their seemingly alien worldview and ethics. For example, in the lectionary's readings for the Sundays after Pentecost, the story of Abraham bargaining with God over the fate of Sodom and Gemorrah (Gen. 18:20-32) is coupled with Jesus teaching his disciples how to pray (Luke 11:20-32). The wisdom literature also seems less moralistic and self-righteous when we read it in the light of Christ, the Wisdom and Word of God. In the lectionary we hear Wisdom calling us to eat her bread and drink her wine and walk in the way of insight (Prov. 9:1-6) as Jesus speaks of himself as the "bread of life" and invites his hearers to eat the flesh and drink the blood of the Son of Man to receive eternal life (John 6:51-58).

Christians have found the prophetic passages in the Hebrew Scriptures more central to contemporary proclamation than have Jews. More of the Old Testament readings in the lectionary are taken from the prophetic books than from the other literary genres. Especially during the Advent/Christmas/Epiphany cycle, there are citations of messianic prophecies, especially from Isaiah (for example, Isa. 2:1-5; 7:10-14; 9:2-7; 11:1-10). Undoubtedly, Isaiah and other prophets were not thinking about Jesus, born some eight centuries later. But the early Christians, reading their words, could only see the fulfillment of prophetic hopes in the life, death, and resurrection of Jesus the Messiah or

Christ. Older texts became sacred Scripture as they were reappropriated, reinterpreted, and read with new insight in new contexts. We see that process at work within the Bible itself. In this process, Scripture interprets Scripture.

If the point of the principle that Scripture interprets Scripture is to say that all Scripture proclaims Christ, this is nowhere truer than in the Psalms. The Letter to the Hebrews proclaims the meaning of the Christ by reference to Psalms 2, 8, 22, and 110. In fact, the whole Christology of Hebrews can be understood as a midrash (commentary) on Psalm 110:4: "You are a priest forever according to the order of Melchizedek." The Psalms not only proclaim Christ; they are sometimes the very words of Christ. Two of the "seven words" of Jesus on the cross are simply citations of the Psalms: "My God, my God, why have you forsaken me" (Ps. 22:1); "Into your hands I commend my spirit" (Ps. 31:5). The christological and typological interpretations of the psalms are evident most especially in the historic Good Friday liturgy. But all the psalms are to be interpreted in these ways, as the Psalter collects in the *Lutheran Book of Worship* Ministers Book and *Evangelical Lutheran Worship* Leaders Edition for use in the daily prayer offices (matins, vespers, compline) endeavor to demonstrate. If the Psalms are about Christ or are the very words of Christ, we are proclaiming Christ or praying with Christ when we sing these words.

The Scriptures live in the church's liturgy. This is their natural home. Those books were canonized as sacred Scriptures that were read in assemblies for worship, first in the synagogue and then in the church. From the moment New Testament readings were added to the Old, a typological interpretation was needed because of the overarching scheme of promise-fulfillment in relationship to the Christ-event.

The Scriptures live within the Church's homiletical practice. Biblical preaching does not expound an idea or even a doctrine; it opens up the scriptures to proclaim Christ, as Jesus opened up the scriptures to proclaim himself to his two disciples on the road to Emmaus (Luke 24:13-27) and as Philip the deacon opened up the scriptures to proclaim Christ to the Ethiopian eunuch (Acts 8:26-39). We note that these acts of proclamation led, respectively, to the Communion meal and to baptism. Biblical sermons proclaim the Christ of the Scriptures and relate our lives to the Christ announced in the word of God and celebrated in the sacraments.

We have critical tools at our disposal today that earlier preachers in the history of the church lacked (although their spiritual insights certainly more than made up for that deficit). By helping us understand the historical and cultural context in which the biblical books were written or in which the events in the biblical narrative took place, by teaching us about the language and history, literature and geography, sociology and archaeology pertaining to the Bible, this method helps us make the biblical events and characters come alive to our people. The real problem with the historical-critical method is that it exacerbates the historical distance between our context and the biblical context. In a real sense, if we are part of the people of God who are the object of the biblical God's work of creation, redemption, and sanctification, then the historical-critical method opens up a chasm within the biblical world itself, since we should be a part of that world.

So the question is, how do we bridge the gap between ourselves and the Bible so that we are consciously a part of the biblical world? One answer is to enter into the liturgy of the church in which Scriptures come alive for us as we make the Bible's words our own in praise and prayer. But another answer is for preachers and teachers to engage in "canonical exegesis," the aim of which is to read individual texts within the context of the Bible as a whole.

Canonical Exegesis

Canonical exegesis interprets the text as it has been received, rather than at the source level (if that can be determined), and as a part of the whole biblical story, rather than as an isolated text. As reclaimed by the late Brevard Childs,[5] canonical exegesis does not ignore historical criticism. But it carries this criticism forward so that the Bible can become the source of doctrine and life. This is not the same as using the Bible as a source of "proof texts" for faith and morals, in which we look for biblical validation of teachings and behaviors. It is a matter of developing teaching and behavior out of the witness of the Bible itself—its total witness—and not imposing other authorities (for example, reason or experience) on the Bible. This is what it means to regard the Bible as the "sole rule and norm" of faith and practice.

In matters of doctrine, for example, the Bible does not teach a doctrine of the Trinity. But its total revelation points to a God who has been named Father, Son, and Holy Spirit (see especially the stories of the baptism of Jesus in Matthew 3:16-17; Mark 1:9-11; Luke 3:21-22; and John 1:31-34). Jesus calls "Father" the One who designates him as "Son," and the Spirit is the bond between them. In matters of sexual ethics, for another example, it is important to understand how biblical stories and teachings placed the conduct of the people of God against the practices of surrounding pagan neighbors, whether in the ancient Near East (Leviticus 18) or in the Roman world of the first century (Romans 1). Historical criticism can help us understand each historical and social context. But developing a moral theology requires taking into account the total witness of the Scriptures in order to discern what God's will is for the people whom God has called to be God's own.

This approach to biblical interpretation also helps us understand anew what biblical inspiration means. We have old pictures of the Holy Spirit whispering in the ears of scribes who sit at their writing desks taking dictation. But inspiration really happens within the covenant relationship of God and God's people. Pope Benedict XVI provides a clue to this more dynamic understanding of inspiration in the introduction to his *Jesus of Nazareth*: "The author does not speak as a private, self-contained subject. He speaks in a living community, that is to say, in a living historical movement not created by him, nor even by the collective, but which is led forward by a greater power that is at work."[6] That is to say, inspiration took place within the historical context of the community of faith just as the process of canonization did. The Bible is the church's book. It was written, edited, and canonized of the church, by the church, and for the church.

Questions for Discussion

1. What is the difference between calling Scripture a "rule and norm" and treating it as a "source" of belief and faith?

2. How do you see Christ in the Old Testament? Consider the story of the sacrifice of Isaac in Genesis 18.

3. Take one of the sets of readings from the lectionary, and compare the Old Testament reading with the gospel reading, looking for typological connections between them.

4. How does "canonical exegesis" help us see the Bible as one unified story about God's relationship with God's people?

3

The Ecumenical Creeds

Besides receiving the canon of Scripture from the Catholic tradition, Lutherans also received from the Church Catholic the three ecumenical creeds: the Apostles' Creed, the Nicene Creed, and the so-called Athanasian Creed. When all of the Lutheran Confessions were gathered together into *The Book of Concord* in 1580, the first section included what were called "The Three Chief Symbols or Creeds of the Christian Faith Which Are Commonly Used in the Church." In the Latin edition of *The Book of Concord,* they are called "The Three Catholic or Ecumenical Symbols." By including these creeds among its confessions of faith, the Lutheran church indicates its commitment to the ancient and ecumenical doctrines of the church.

The church develops creeds or confessions of faith when the faithful are uncertain about what to believe. Early Christians may have had to sort out how their belief in Jesus related to Jewish monotheism and pagan polytheism. The earliest creed, "Jesus is *Kyrios* (Greek: *Lord*)," may have dealt with both of these concerns, since Jewish Christians could understand by this statement that "Jesus is Yahweh" (and therefore divine as well as human) and Gentile Christians could understand that Jesus is *Dominus* (Latin: *Lord*), even though the emperor claimed that title and divinity).

Of course, the greatest source of confusion to ordinary believers has come from within the Christian community itself when there is disagreement over basic beliefs. In early Christianity, Gnosticism was a major source of confusion. Gnosticism was not a religion in itself as much as a mind-set that pervaded Hellenistic culture in the early Christian era. There were Christian teachers who imbibed the gnostic spirit and attracted followers by their seeming expertise in biblical exegesis. They dug through the Scriptures to mine nuggets of spiritual wisdom. Just as gnostics assumed that the meaning of Jesus lay in his divine reality apart from his concrete historicity as a Jewish male, so they assumed that the theological value of a biblical text lay at some spiritual level other than the raw narrative or legal code. Gnostics especially prized those areas in which the biblical narrative was silent, such as the thirty years of Jesus' life between his infancy and the beginning of his ministry. From their private sources of revelation they posited thirty aeons that provided clues to the history of the world. Other gnostics produced their own scriptures (such as the gospels found in the Nag Hammadi Library) or decided that certain writings weren't worth reading in the liturgical assembly.

Among the latter was the teacher Marcion, who disavowed the value of the Hebrew Scriptures and recognized as authentic only an expurgated version of the Gospel according to Luke and the ten authentic letters of Paul. Against the gnostics, who may have been inundating Gaul, Bishop Irenaeus of Lyons, toward the end of the second century, provided three legs to support the teaching authority of orthodoxy: bishops in apostolic succession, a canon of Sacred Scripture, and a rule of faith. Against teachers with their own private pipeline of apostolic teaching, Irenaeus produced lists of bishops in succession from the apostles, so as to say, "We know from whom we received our information. There is no secret knowledge here." The apostles told their successors what they needed to know about Jesus the Christ, and they wrote down (or caused to be written down) their witness to the good news of salvation in Christ. So Irenaeus proposed a canon of four apostolic gospels in opposition to Marcion's one gospel. The church must receive the fullness of the apostolic witness to Christ, discrepancies and all. We can live with the discrepancies in the narrative if we know what is most fundamental to the plot. This plot summary is provided by a rule of faith that, in Irenaeus' *Against the Heresies*, looks very much like the first and second articles of the later Apostles' Creed.

The Apostles' Creed

Since Irenaeus mentions that "many barbarian peoples who believe in Christ follow this rule," we may assume that this "rule of faith" had been around for a while. Indeed, it was probably what new Christians had professed at their baptism. The triple profession of faith included in the baptismal liturgy, provided in *The Apostolic Tradition* attributed to Hippolytus of Rome (approximately A.D. 215), looks even more like the Apostles' Creed. In the form provided by "Hippolytus," the candidates responded to each of three questions—"Do you believe" in God the Father, in Jesus Christ the Son of God, and in the Holy Spirit in the holy church?—with "I believe," and were dipped in the water after each profession.

That a creed similar to the Apostles' Creed was circulating throughout the church in the third and fourth centuries is suggested by the legend reported in the Syrian *Apostolic Constitutions* (about 380) describing how each of the apostles contributed a phrase to this creed. This legend was already exposed as false in the fifth century, but the name "Apostles" stuck to this creed because it is such a basic statement of the apostolic proclamation, or *kerygma*. The full text of the creed as we know it does not appear until the eighth century in manuscripts copied in southern France. But the Apostles' Creed was most likely being used in the Roman and Gallican Churches in the previous centuries, especially for catechetical purposes, because of its brevity and clarity.

The simplicity of this creed should not lead one to think that it lacks depth. Each phrase packs a powerful theological statement. God is called "Father almighty." These words together suggest both the immanence and transcendence of God. God is "the maker of heaven and earth," which rejects any idea that God is a part of creation.

Jesus Christ is identified as "God's only Son" and "our Lord." Sonship expresses Jesus' relationship with the Father. "Lord" expresses his relationship to his disciples. "Conceived by the Holy Spirit" and "born of the Virgin Mary" express Jesus' true divinity and humanity in concrete terms. "Suffered under Pontius Pilate" locates the Son of God in human history. "Suffered . . . crucified, died, and was buried" describes the event of the passion without specifying its meaning. "He descended into hell" was not in the older Roman form of the creed. It is likely based on 1 Peter 3:19 and 4:6 and has been interpreted to mean variously that Christ preached in the abode of the dead during his three days in the tomb, or that he released the Old Testament saints from the devil's captivity, or that he conquered Satan. It may simply mean that he was dead and has been interpreted this way in contemporary translations: "he descended to the dead." The resurrection on the third day and the ascension into heaven, along with Jesus' session at the right hand of God the Father almighty, proclaim him as the living and reigning Lord. Christ's return to judge the living and the dead would be something important for catechumens to consider.

Belief in the Holy Spirit also entails belief in "the holy catholic church, the communion of saints, the forgiveness of sins, the resurrection of the body, and the life everlasting." These are the works of the Holy Spirit, as Luther would interpret them in his explanation of the third article. The Spirit creates the church, in which sins are daily forgiven, and raises up the child of God to new and eternal life. The "communion of saints" is ambiguously masculine or neuter in Latin. If *communio sanctorum* is masculine, it refers to "holy people" (saints); if it is neuter, it refers to "holy things" (sacraments). In a text as dense as this, it is unlikely that "communion of saints" is simply a synonym for "holy catholic church." Early medieval believers would have certainly understood a reference to holy people to mean the saints in heaven. Conversely, the lack of reference to baptism in the Apostles' Creed (such as there is in the Nicene Creed) suggests that this phrase refers to holy things. We might note that the creed does not mention the Greek idea of the immortality of the soul, only the clear biblical idea of the resurrection of the body.

The Nicene Creed

Unlike the Apostles' Creed, which emerged in widely scattered local congregations for use with candidates for baptism, the Nicene Creed was written at a specific time and place to deal with a specific situation. Only a dozen years after Christianity became a legal cult in the Roman Empire through the Edict of Milan (313), Emperor Constantine assembled the Christian bishops of the Roman Empire to his summer palace at Nicaea (325). The purpose of this gathering was to agree on what the church teaches and what Christians are to believe in the face of conflicting beliefs that were confusing the faithful and dividing the church (which the emperor hoped would unify and renew the empire). The bishops began their deliberations by placing on the table their local baptismal professions of faith. Among the heresies that needed to be addressed by the Nicene fathers was Arianism, which put at stake the whole reality of Jesus as *Savior* in its teaching that Jesus was a created being and that, although he might be called "the Son of God," he does not share in the being or essence of God and is therefore subordinate to the Father. In the aphorism attributed to Athanasius, "What has not been assumed has not been redeemed," the idea is that if God did not become man and enter fully into human life, we have no assurance that human life has been redeemed. It is likely that the bishops agreed on one local baptismal creed that could serve as a framework for establishing what "we believe," and added to this the controversial term *homoousion* ("of one being") to affirm the substantial unity of the Father and the Son.[1]

The creed affirmed belief in "one God" in order to avoid any suggestion of tritheism in its doctrine of the Trinity. The crucial article in the creed as promulgated by the Council of Nicea is the second. It was necessary to affirm the full divinity of Christ in order to affirm God as Trinity. The Arians could accept Jesus' unique role as Son of God, Christ, and Lord. What they could not accept was the Son's equal divinity with the Father. Hence phrases are heaped up that confess the Lord Jesus Christ as "God of God, Light of Light, true God of true God, begotten not made, of one being (*homoousion*) with the Father." With this affirmed, the creed goes on to speak of salvation by means of the incarnation of the eternal Son of God as "man."

The promulgation of this creed did not bring about unity but led to greater strife and division as the Arians fought back against the "novelty" perpetrated at Nicaea. Alexandria especially was a hotbed of Arianism (Arius had been a presbyter or priest of that church), and Bishop Athanasius was deposed by emperors five times because of his defense of Nicene orthodoxy. A second ecumenical council had to be convened in Constantinople in 381 (when Gregory of Nazianzus was bishop in the imperial capital) to reaffirm the Creed of Nicaea and shore up belief in the divinity of the Holy Spirit, which had become controverted in the meantime. The Nicene-Constantinopolian Creed affirms the deity of the Holy Spirit by saying that the Spirit is worthy to be "worshiped and glorified." While the Son is "begotten" of the Father, the Spirit "proceeds" from the Father. The Western church would later add that the Spirit "proceeds from the Father and the Son" (*filioque*), which would become a matter of contention between the Eastern and the Western church, since the East would claim that the West had no authority to add something to a text agreed upon by an ecumenical council. The second ecumenical council also added the adjectives *one* and *apostolic* to *holy* and *catholic* as marks of the church. There can be only one church if there is one truth, and this truth is founded on the apostolic witness.

The two great issues that the Nicene-Constantinopolitan Creed had to sort out were the doctrines of God and of the Christ. The Christian doctrine of God is the concept of Trinity, three persons in one being. The doctrine of Christ was expressed in terms of two natures in one person that are equally divine and human. The purpose of the creed was to establish the perimeters of belief, not to explain the mystery of the Godhead or of the incarnation. Theologians could work on their explanations since faith is always seeking understanding (as Anselm later put it). But they could not stray outside this perimeter.

The Athanasian Creed

The Athanasian Creed, properly named the *Quicunque vult salvus esse* ("Whoever wishes to be saved") is a creed that has been used as a canticle (liturgical song). Indeed, it begins not by saying, "We believe," but, "We worship one God in three persons and three persons in one God." In spite of its name, this creed certainly cannot be attributed to Athanasius of Alexandria; theologically, it is more akin to the Trinitarian theology of Augustine of Hippo.

Just as the Nicene Creed has been recited (chanted) in the Mass or eucharistic liturgy (more on that later in this chapter), so the *Quicunque vult* has been chanted antiphonally (two sides singing back and forth to each other) in the monastic prayer office of prime (the first gathering for prayer after breakfast). Its use in prime at the beginning of the day suggests the value of this creed as a teaching document. Its repetition of phrases (see the text in *Lutheran Book of Worship*, pp. 54-55) nails down the Trinity so that there will be no danger of "confusing the persons" (the modalist heresy, which viewed the three members of the Trinity as different modes of God's activity rather than as separate persons) or "dividing the divine substance" (the Arian heresy, described in the discussion of the Nicene Creed). Whatever one divine person is—uncreated, infinite, eternal, almighty—that is what the other two persons are. There are not three gods but one God, and not three lords but one Lord. Yet there are also differences among the divine persons. The Father is unoriginate; the Son is begotten; the Spirit proceeds (the *filioque* is affirmed in this Western creed), and there is one Father, one Son, one Holy Spirit. Far from being a complicated creed, it is very simpleminded.

The second part of the Athanasian Creed confesses the two natures of Christ as both God and man, "begotten before all worlds from the being of the Father" yet "born in the world from the being of his mother." Christ exists fully as God and fully as man, yet the two natures are not to be confused. In the recitation of salvation history in the Christ-story, the descent into hell also is affirmed.

At the beginning and ending are statements that strike the modern Christian as intolerant and maybe intolerable: "Whoever wants to be saved should above all cling to the catholic faith. Whoever does not guard it whole and inviolable will doubtless perish eternally." And, at the end: "This is the catholic faith. One cannot be saved without believing this firmly and faithfully." The creed affirms that there is no way to salvation apart from Christ. Even the good works that merit salvation are those works performed, knowingly or unknowingly, for Christ himself "just as you did it to one of the least of these . . ." (Matt. 25:40). What merits condemnation is not ignorance of this catholic faith, but rejection of it.

The *Te Deum Laudamus*

If the *Quicinque vult* is a creed that has been used as a canticle, the *Te Deum laudamus* ("We praise you, O God") is a canticle that has been used as a creed (see the text in *Lutheran Book of Worship*, pp. 139-41). In 1537 Martin Luther wrote a forty-eight-page pamphlet entitled *The Three Symbols or Confessions of the Faith of Christ Used Unanimously in the Church* (published in 1538). The first of these "confessions" is the Apostles' Creed, and the second is the so-called Athanasian Creed, but Luther says of the third, "The third symbol is supposed to be St. Augustine's and St. Ambrose's and to have been sung after St. Augustine's baptism. Whether that be true or not, no harm is done if one believes it to have been the case. For whoever the author is, it is a fine symbol or confession, written in the form of a canticle to enable us not only to confess the true faith but also to give thanks to God in the process."[2] He is referring to the Te Deum. Luther's acceptance of these three as the chief symbols does not in any way depreciate the Nicene Creed. Luther provided a translation of that creed in an appendix and reported, "It is sung every Sunday."

The legend that the Te Deum was jointly inspired by Augustine and Ambrose at the former's baptism is certainly unreliable. We know that the text was cited at the end of the fifth century by Caesarius of Arles, a monk of the Mediterranean island monastery of Lérins. Scholars now believe that it was originally a baptismal hymn, perhaps sung in the procession to the font at the Vigil of Easter Eve, which in the fifth century was still the primary time of the church year for baptisms. Later on, the Litany of the Saints was sung in the procession to the font, and in the Easter Vigil in the *Lutheran Book of Worship*, the Song of the Three Children (*Benedicite opera omnia*) concludes the final reading as the congregation gathers around the font. Like these other texts, the Te Deum invokes cosmic references: "the glorious company of the apostles," "the noble fellowship of prophets," "the white-robed army of martyrs," "the holy Church throughout the world." It is also a marvelous statement of salvation in Christ addressed to Christ: In order to take on our humanity, you did not spurn the virgin's womb; in order to open the kingdom of heaven to all believers, you overcame the sting of death; in order to share the divine might and power as a human being as well as God, you sit at the right hand of God the Father; in order to vindicate your people and claim your own, you will come again as judge.

Orthodox Doxology

In the wake of the Arian controversy of the fourth and fifth centuries, Christian liturgy began to reflect the decisions of Nicaea and Constantinople (and one can imagine the "worship wars" that took place). According to Josef Jungmann, when the Arians appealed to the consistent reference to Christ's role as mediator in catholic prayer ("through Jesus Christ our Lord") to "prove" that the Son is subordinate to the Father, the anti-Arians responded by adding words to the prayer endings to stress the co-equality of the three Persons of the one Godhead: "who lives and reigns with the Father and the Holy Spirit, one God, now and forever."[3] They also terminated psalms and canticles with words of praise called doxologies.

In the East, a typical doxology was that proposed by Basil the Great: "Glory to the Father *with* (*meta*) the Son *together with* (*syn*) the Holy Spirit." In the West, the little doxology appended to psalms and canticles was also altered to express the co-equality of the three Persons of the Trinity: "Glory to the Father and to the Son and to the Holy Spirit." The precise wording of this "lesser doxology" (*Gloria Patri*) was fixed at the Council of Vaison in 529. All of the classic Latin hymns, beginning with those of Ambrose of Milan in the late fourth century, have a full Trinitarian doxology as the final stanza praising the Father, the Son, and the Holy Spirit.

Not only prayer terminations and concluding doxologies, but the whole historic liturgy was addressed either to the Trinity or to Christ. The *Kyrie eleison* (Lord have mercy) is addressed to Christ, as is indicated by the alternation with *Christe eleison* (Christ have mercy). The greater Gloria (*Gloria in excelsis*) is both Trinitarian and christological. After the citation of Luke 2:14 (the song of the angels announcing the birth of Christ), it begins, "Lord God, heavenly king, almighty God and Father; we worship you, we give you thanks, we praise you for your glory." But the second part is addressed to "Lord Jesus Christ, only Son of the Father." Likewise, the Te Deum begins, "We praise you, O God, we acknowledge you to be the Lord." The second part begins, "You, Christ, are the king of glory." We should note that these songs in the Western liturgy, along with the *Quicunque vult*, occurred as the church in the Western Roman Empire battled theologically the Arianism of the Gothic tribes who were invading and settling down in northern Italy, Gaul, Spain, and north Africa.

Reciting the Creed

I have referred several times to reciting a creed in the liturgy. (Before modern times, "reciting" a liturgical text usually meant chanting it.) The Nicene-Constantinopolitan Creed was first introduced into the Liturgy of Constantinople during the patriarchate of Timothy (511–517), who was accused of monophysite tendencies (the teaching that there was one divine nature in the human person of Jesus), in order to assert his orthodoxy.[4] This use of the creed in the Divine Liturgy spread quickly throughout the East, except among the Nestorians (followers of Nestorius, who emphasized the humanity of Christ) east of the Byzantine Empire. The Byzantine use of the creed in the liturgy may be seen as one of several liturgical innovations that exalted the divinity of Christ, including the *Monogenes* (Only-begotten) hymn and the *Trisagion* (Thrice-Holy), which also date from this period.

The original anti-Arian purpose of the Nicene Creed returned to the fore in Spain. The occasion was the conversion of the Visigothic king Recared from Arianism to Catholicism in 589. The Council of Toledo decreed that the creed should be recited by the faithful at every mass. This recapitulatory use of the creed (that is, reciting it regularly in the liturgy) spread into the Frankish Kingdom at the end of the eighth century. The German emperor Henry II was surprised to find the creed missing from the Roman Mass when he visited Rome in 1014. Pope Benedict VIII argued that the Roman Church had never been afflicted by heresy and therefore did not need to repeat the creed so often, but agreed under pressure that the creed would henceforth be recited on Sundays and major feast days. This liturgical use of the creed continues in the Eastern Orthodox, Roman Catholic, Lutheran, Anglican, and some Reformed traditions.

It is very important that only these creeds and no others be recited (spoken or sung) in public worship. The substance of our ecumenical creeds goes back to apostolic times, and their precise formulations go back to the patristic era. They are affirmations of a faith that has been tested and achieved consensus in the ecumenical church. That cannot be said of affirmations of faith that are developed in local congregations or even in particular denominations. When in Holy Baptism the believer professes his or her faith, he or she is being initiated into a people of God who are grounded in the Christ who is "the same yesterday, today, and forever" (Heb. 13:8). As long as the believer continues to repeat this confession, he or she may be assured of his or her identification with the Christian people. Also, in the welter of denominations and independent congregations in America today, the Christian believer may at least assume that an assembly that recites the creed is an orthodox church. The creeds are called "symbols" because they provide the identity of faith, just as a flag identifies a country or an army. The individual believer is able to find his or her ecumenical identity and solidarity with the church catholic when one of the ancient ecumenical creeds is recited in the liturgy.

Questions for Discussion

1. Are ancient heresies that deny Christ's humanity (Gnosticism) or divinity (Arianism) evident in the world today?

2. How do the creeds help us sort out what we believe about God and about Christ?

3. How do praying and singing lead to belief? Are how we pray and what we sing important?

4. Do you agree that contemporary affirmations of faith should not replace the ancient ecumenical creeds? What is gained by using contemporary affirmations? What is lost?

4

The Lutheran Confessions

We come now to something in Lutheran identity that is distinctly Lutheran: our confessions or symbolical books. However, before we get too deep into matters that are the unique Lutheran witness, we should note that the confessions themselves resist claiming anything new. The summary of the doctrinal articles 1–21 in the Augsburg Confession claims, "There is nothing here that departs from the Scriptures or the catholic church or the church of Rome, in so far as the ancient church is known to us from its writers."[1] The summary of the articles about practical matters in dispute (articles 22–28) also affirms, "Nothing has been received among us, in doctrine or in ceremonies, that is contrary to Scripture or to the church catholic. For it is manifest that we have guarded diligently against the introduction into our churches of any new and ungodly doctrines."[2] As a way of demonstrating the confessors' commitment to the great tradition of the catholic faith, they condemn by name all the heresies that were condemned by ancient councils. The articles of the Augsburg Confession are studded with citations from the church fathers as well as from Scripture.

The Augsburg Confession

Certainly, there was interest in being as conciliatory as possible at the Diet of Augsburg in 1530. The Holy Roman Emperor, Charles V, had convened the diet to try to resolve the religious controversies in order to mount a united imperial front against the Ottoman Turks, who were advancing up the Danube and were near the gates of Vienna. The Hapsburg emperor, born in the Low Countries and also king of Spain, was an ardent Catholic but recognized the need for reform in the church. He was not always on good terms with the papacy. The princes and free cities that had embraced the Lutheran reform movement during the 1520s had an opportunity to advance their agenda for reform. Hence they affirmed irenically, "We on our part shall not omit doing anything, in so far as God and conscience allow, that may serve the cause of Christian unity."[3]

Even so, they realized that Martin Luther had gone beyond other Reformers in attacking the *teachings* that lay behind bad practices. The Lutheran princes and magistrates realized that they had to present their theological issues in as positive a light as possible. It was the job of Philipp Melanchthon, Luther's younger colleague at the University of Wittenberg, to take the articles that various territories had drafted and weld them into a statement that was both theologically pointed and practically defensible. As one with humanist sympathies, he could do this with an appeal to the great tradition, the teachings of the church fathers, and the empirical reality of church life.

Thus, the Augsburg Confession, which was written by Melanchthon, not Luther, builds to its central dogmatic proposal[4] by laying the groundwork of the well-established catholic dogmas of the Holy Trinity, original sin, and the two natures of Christ (articles 1–3). Article 1 is a restatement of the classical Trinitarian faith. Article 2 appropriates a definition of original sin derived from Thomas Aquinas, who had based it on certain formulations of Augustine, and adds a conventional condemnation of Pelagianism. (Pelagianism, the teaching of the fifth-century monk Pelagius, holds that people are free to choose good or evil because there is no inherited sin from Adam; infants are born in the same condition as Adam and Eve before the fall and become sinners only by violating the moral law. This view was condemned by the Council of Ephesus in 431.) Article 3 amounts to little more than a reformulation of the Apostles' Creed, to which it also refers. It also draws upon an understanding of Christ as the victim of the atoning sacrifice that was standard in the catholic tradition.

Thus, articles 1–3 seek to establish a common doctrinal basis between Rome and the Reformers that lays the groundwork for the crucial article 4: justification by faith. Jaroslav Pelikan put the theological logic this way: "If the Holy Trinity was as holy as the Trinitarian dogma taught; if original sin was as virulent as the Augustinian tradition said it was; and if Christ was as necessary as the Christological dogma implied—then the only way to treat justification in a manner faithful to the best of Catholic tradition was to teach justification by faith."[5] As a basis for their core theological proposal, the confessors cite Romans 3:21-26 and 4:5.

> Our churches also teach that men cannot be justified before God by their own strength, merits, or works but are freely justified for Christ's sake through faith when they believe that they are received into favor and that their sins are forgiven on account of Christ, who by his death made satisfaction for our sins. This faith God imputes for righteousness in his sight (Romans 3, 4).

The word "alone" (*sola*) that Luther purportedly wrote into the margin of the Bible when he read Romans 3:19, "we hold that a person is justified by faith," is not present in either the German or the Latin text of article 4 of the Augsburg Confession. But *sola fide* is implied in the articles that follow. Everything taught and practiced in the church serves to proclaim Christ and elicit faith in him.

The first twenty-one articles deal with doctrine, about which the confessors said there should be no controversy because these teachings conform to Scripture and the catholic tradition. There follow seven "Articles in which an account is given of the abuses which have been corrected." These articles deal with the reform of Communion practices, the end of enforced clerical celibacy, the abolition of votive masses, the pastoral use of individual confession, the easing of fasting requirements, a reconsideration of monastic vows, and the distinction between temporal and spiritual power. On the last point, the confessors held that evangelical bishops should preach the gospel, judge doctrine, administer the sacraments, and visit parishes. Where bishops exercise temporal power, it is not on the basis of the Word alone but human custom.

Content of *The Book of Concord*

The Augsburg Confession is the primary Lutheran statement of faith. This and the other Lutheran confessions are collected into *The Book of Concord* (1580). They include the three Chief Symbols (the ecumenical creeds); the Augsburg Confession (1530); the *Apology of the Augsburg Confession* (1531); the Smalcald Articles (1537); the *Treatise on the Power and Primacy of the Pope* (1537), appended to the Smalcald Articles; the *Small Catechism* of Martin Luther (1529); the *Large Catechism* of Martin Luther (1529); the Formula of Concord (1577); and *A Catalogue of Testimonies of the Church Fathers* (1577), prepared by Martin Chemnitz, appended to the Formula of Concord.

The *Apology of the Augsburg Confession*

Charles V might have been impressed by the irenic tone of the Augsburg Confession because he rejected more hostile replies to it. But finally a draft *Confutation of the Augsburg Confession* was prepared that satisfied the emperor and was read in German before the diet. The Lutherans were given neither a copy nor an opportunity to respond to it. But careful notes were taken, and Philipp Melanchthon prepared a response, the *Apology or Defense of the Augsburg Confession*, which goes into great detail, especially concerning the articles on which the Roman party objected. The scholarship of the *Apology* is impressive, especially in terms of biblical and patristic citations. It was published, together with the confession in 1531, and gave great encouragement to the Lutheran movement.

Of particular interest in the *Apology* is the development of Luther's distinction between law and gospel. In the *Apology*, Melanchthon expresses Luther's clarity on law and gospel as he responds to the *Confutation's* objections to the doctrine of justification. In nineteenth-century American Lutheranism, the Missouri Synod leader C. F. W. Walther gave a series of vehement lectures on this topic. For Luther, for Melanchthon, and most certainly for Walther, there is a clear polemical note in their adumbrations of the law-gospel distinction. Walther even ups the ante of orthodoxy by saying, "Only he is an orthodox teacher who not only presents all the articles of faith in accordance with Scripture, but also rightly distinguishes from each other the Law and the Gospel."[6] From that comes the bald assertion that any teacher who fails in this task of rightly distinguishing law and gospel in practice has lapsed into heretical teaching. At the heart of this assertion is a pastoral issue. Pastoral care will be rightly practiced only when it flows from a consistent apprehension of the twin messages of Scripture: law and gospel—what God requires of us and what God gives to us as an act of grace. It is because of the consistency of these two themes that right pastoral care seems to display an inconsistency, reading the law to one person and giving the consolation of the gospel to the troubled conscience of another person.

The Smalcald Articles

When Pope Paul III called for a general council of the church to address the controversies generated by the Reformation, Elector John Frederick of Saxony requested that Martin Luther prepare a response. He complied by drafting the Smalcald Articles, named after the city in which the Lutheran theologians met. This document more firmly states the Lutheran position on controverted doctrinal articles, pointing out those articles of faith on which no compromise can be made but also noting articles on which there could be concessions. The Smalcald Articles state that the doctrine of justification by faith is "the article on which the church stands or falls," about which there can be no compromise. Because the Roman church had rejected this article concerning the very heart of the gospel, Luther declared that the pope was the Antichrist, and that a general council should be convened under the presidency of the emperor rather than the pope to condemn the Roman error.

Appended to the Smalcald Articles is a *Treatise on the Power and Primacy of the Pope*, prepared by Melanchthon, in which the "Praeceptor (Teacher) of Germany" (the honorary title bestowed on Melanchthon because of his reforms of the university) denied the papal claims of supremacy over the church by divine right, of supremacy over the kingdoms by divine right, and that all Christians must believe in this supremacy and submit to the pope. In a codicil, however, Melanchthon wrote that the pope could be regarded as a universal bishop by human right for the sake of Christian unity.

The Catechisms

The Small Catechism and *The Large Catechism* of Martin Luther were produced in response to the deplorable situation he discovered during his visitation of parishes in Electoral Saxony in 1528. Some peasants wouldn't learn the Our Father—the Lord's Prayer—because it was too long. There were priests who could not recite the Apostles' Creed. Some parishioners had not received Holy Communion in years. Referring to the visitations that inspired these works, Luther wrote in the preface to *The Small Catechism*, "Good God, what wretchedness I beheld! The common people, especially those who live in the country, have no knowledge whatever of Christian teaching, and unfortunately many pastors are quite incompetent and unfitted for teaching."[7] In his catechisms, Luther dealt with the very basics of the Christian faith: the Ten Commandments, the Apostles' Creed, the Lord's Prayer, and the sacraments of baptism, confession and absolution, and Holy Communion. He also provided simple forms of morning and evening prayer, grace at table (based on the table prayers Luther had learned in the monastery), and a table of household duties.

The Small Catechism was to be used by heads of households, pastors, and teachers for the instruction of children. Luther insisted that the texts should be memorized and not changed from year to year. *The Large Catechism* was intended to teach the teachers. Those who would not learn the catechism should be told that they are not Christians and be forbidden to serve as sponsors at baptism or come to Holy Communion. In the preface to the *The Large Catechism*, Luther admonished pastors and teachers to learn the catechism, pointing out that he, too, though a doctor of the church, "must remain a child and pupil of the Catechism, and I do it gladly."[8] He admonished all Christians to study the catechism constantly and to put it into practice.

The Large Catechism was based on a series of sermons Luther had preached on the catechism in 1528. Sermons on the catechism became a standard Lutheran practice, and some of these became the substance of other catechisms. One of the most popular of these other catechisms was the *Catechism or Children's Sermons* published in Nuremberg in 1533.[9] It was undoubtedly the work primarily of Nuremberg's chief pastor and reformer, Andreas Osiander. These homilies elaborated on Luther's *The Small Catechism* for youth between the ages of twelve and fourteen who were preparing for their first Holy Communion. The reason for the public-sermon format was the success of catechesis in this first officially Lutheran city. Some twelve hundred youth were being prepared each year for First Communion in the city's Saint Sebaldus and Saint Lorenz churches alone, far too many for the small number of the city's pastors to provide individual or small-group instruction.

The Nuremberg catechism became a best seller throughout Germany. It was translated into Latin by Justus Jonas. The reforming archbishop of Canterbury, Thomas Cranmer, who had married Osiander's niece, had the Latin version translated into English as a handbook for priests in 1548. The catechism in the Church Order of Archbishop Hermann von Wied, elector of Cologne, prepared jointly by Martin Bucer and Philipp Melanchthon, also was translated into English along with the rest of the church order, under the title *A Pious and Religious Consultation* (1548). These German catechisms became the basis of the catechism in the *Prayer Book of King Edward VI* (1549). The *Prayer Book* catechism serves as the basis of the bishop's examination of children before confirmation. A rubric specifies that at least once every six weeks, the priest is to provide instruction and examination on some part of the catechism with preconfirmation children.

The Rite of Confirmation

Because the rite of confirmation for youth has been an important part of Lutheran identity, it seems appropriate to insert an excursus on it here. It may surprise many Lutherans to know that Luther regarded confirmation as so much "monkey business" (*affenspiel*) and provided no suggestions for a rite. He was reacting to the medieval practice of confirmation, which many liturgists have called "a practice in search of a theory." He didn't regard episcopal confirmation (only a bishop could perform confirmations) as a sacrament instituted by Christ, and he certainly didn't want a rite of confirmation competing with baptism. Confirmation by bishops was one of the rites restored during the Leipzig Interim in 1548, when the emperor imposed some pre-Reformation practices on subjugated territories with Melanchthon's blessing after the Smalcald War, that instigated the Adiaphoristic Controversy (described later in this chapter in the discussion of the Formula of Concord). However, Luther was very much in favor of catechetical instruction, and in Lutheran and Reformed practice, it was a prelude to First Communion. For that matter, most communicants were quizzed on the catechism, as well as shriven (examined concerning their life) when they announced their intention to receive the sacrament. What mattered to Luther was the content of faith, not a rite that was believed to "complete" baptism.

Martin Bucer developed an evangelical rite of confirmation at Strassburg to counter the accusation of the Anabaptists that the magisterial Reformation was lax in church discipline. He and Melanchthon provided a rite of confirmation for the church order of Archbishop Hermann. But a real rite of confirmation did not develop in the Lutheran church until the Age of Enlightenment in the eighteenth century, when rationalist churchmen taught that it was important for youth baptized in infancy to make their own personal affirmation of faith. In the cultural Christianity of the time, confirmation was also regarded as a rite of passage into adulthood and citizenship.

As previously noted, however, for Lutherans, as for those in other traditions, confirmation has been a practice in search of a theory. Some Lutherans taught that baptism makes one a member of the Christian Church, whereas confirmation makes one a member of the Lutheran Church. More recently, confirmation has been construed as an affirmation of baptism. This designation testifies that confirmation should never take priority over the premier sacrament of holy baptism in one's Christian life.

God's Work in Baptism

Luther treats the sacrament of holy baptism in both *The Small Catechism* and *The Large Catechism*. In Robert Kolb and Timothy

Wengert's edition of *The Book of Concord*, they include with *The Small Catechism* Luther's *Baptismal Booklet: Translated into German and Newly Revised* (1526). Luther put the order of baptism into the vernacular (1523) even before he produced a vernacular Mass and order of Holy Communion (1526). This was because he found that people were not treating the sacrament of holy baptism with the seriousness that it deserved. He thought they should understand why it is so important to bring their children to baptism as soon as possible. Baptism is a washing of regeneration (new birth). Human beings born into the fallen condition of sin and subject to death and the power of the devil need the deliverance that baptism provides. That is why Luther retained the exorcism in his order of baptism, because only by God's power can we be loosed from the power of the devil. This became a great controversy between Lutherans and the Reformed, who believed that the exorcism was a leftover bit of popish mumbo jumbo. Against the Reformed, the Lutherans emphasized exorcism in baptism all the more vociferously. Against Anabaptists and others who regarded baptism as a work that human beings do, an outward sign of one's belief in Christ, Luther emphasized in *The Large Catechism* that baptism is not our work, but God's work. "To be baptized in God's name is to be baptized not by men but by God himself. Although it is performed by men's hands, it is nevertheless truly God's own act."[10]

This is also why Luther defended the appropriateness of infant baptism in *The Large Catechism*. Against those who would practice only what later came to be called "believer's baptism," Luther argued that the baptism of infants is pleasing to God because "God has sanctified many who have been thus baptized and has given them the Holy Spirit" (see Titus 3:5-8). Furthermore, one's belief is not as important as God's word and command to baptize all nations (Matt. 20:16). Finally, the baptizing community baptizes in the faith that God's promises are trustworthy. In *The Small Catechism*, Luther cites Mark 16:16: "The one who believes and is baptized will be saved; but the one who does not believe will be condemned."

In *The Small Catechism*, Luther sets out baptism not just as a momentary rite but as a lifelong way of life. Baptism "signifies that the old creature in us with all sins and evil desires is to be drowned and die through daily contrition and repentance, and on the other hand that daily a new person is to come forth and rise up to live before God in righteousness and purity forever."[11] In *The Large Catechism,* he writes, "Let all Christians regard their baptism as the daily garment that they are to wear all the time. Every day they should be found in faith and with its fruits, suppressing the old creature and growing up in the new."[12]

The Formula of Concord

In the years after Luther's death in 1546, theological disputes arose among his followers. Some disputes were caused by various responses to the crisis of the Smalcald War (1546–1548), the defeat of the Lutheran princes by the emperor, and the resulting "interims," in which the emperor reimposed pre-Reformation practices in Lutheran territories while waiting for practices to be sorted out in a general council. Melanchthon felt there could be concessions as long as the chief doctrine of justification by faith remained. In contrast, Matthias Flacius of Magdeburg held, "In a state of confession nothing is an indifferent matter (*adiaphoron*)." Their differing perspectives became known as the Adiaphoristic Controversy. Other controversies arose because some teachers took Luther's position on the freedom of the Christian in too extreme a direction (the Antinomian Controversy). Still other disputes arose because some of Luther's followers tried to reach agreement on the Lord's Supper with the Calvinists (the Crypto-Calvinist Controversy). Still other theologians taught doctrines that compromised justification by faith alone through grace (the Synergistic Controversy, the Majoristic Controversy, and the Osiandrian Controversy).

The Peace of Augsburg in 1555 gave equal status to the Lutheran and Catholic churches in the territories of the Holy Roman Empire under the principle *eius regio eius religio* (to each ruler his religion). Lutheranism had become an established church. It was necessary as a political matter for Lutheranism to get its confessional act together, not just over against the Catholics on the one hand and the Reformed on the other, but also to be able to say which church is Lutheran.

To some extent, the controversies involved personality clashes. The usually irenic Melanchthon, who had endorsed the practices of the interim for the sake of peace and as long as core doctrines were not compromised, would not be reconciled with the usually acerbic Matthias Flacius, even though Flacius made many conciliatory offers. But as the main antagonists of these disputes died off, it became possible for the second generation to work out the settlement of theological controversies. The result of this settlement was the Formula of Concord (1577). The leading theologians behind this formidable task included Jacob Andreae, David Chytraeus, and Martin Chemnitz (often called "the second Martin").

The process began in 1576, when Elector August of Saxony convened a conference of theologians at Torgau. The conference drew up the *Torgau Book*, which Andreae summarized in the epitome that was circulated throughout Germany. The following year, at the Bergen Abbey, the *Torgau Book* was reworked into the section of the Formula called "The Solid Declaration." Melanchthon and his disciples were big losers in the settlements of the Adiaphoristic and Crypto-Calvinist controversies, but Melanchthon's neo-scholastic theological method was enshrined in the Formula of Concord as the first major document of post-Reformation Lutheran orthodoxy. Over the next three years, while the preface went through draft after draft, more than eight thousand theologians, pastors, and teachers signed the Solid Declaration. Finally, on June 25, 1580, fifty years from the day when the Augsburg Confession had been presented, the complete *Book of Concord* was available for sale.

The Formula does not discuss all the articles of doctrine, but only those that were controverted. It offered a consensus that had been reached on the basis of the word of God. Hence, the Formula is introduced by a statement that "the sole rule and norm" by which all teachers and teachings are evaluated and judged are the prophetic and apostolic writings of the Old and New Testaments, which are referred to as "God's Word." Yet the Scriptures are not the only source of doctrine or practice. The three ecumenical creeds are accepted as valid testimonies against errors and heresies. In addition, the Augsburg

Confession and its Apology are recognized as true interpretations of Scripture. The Formula is explicit that it accepts only the 1530 version of the Augsburg Confession, not the 1540 *variata* version prepared by Melanchthon in an effort to achieve agreement with the Calvinists on the Lord's Supper. Melanchthon is not even mentioned by name in the formula; all loyalty is to Martin Luther alone as the great prophet of the Reformation. The catechisms of Luther are held up as "the layman's Bible"; the Formula addresses theologians. The doctrinal unanimity achieved by the Formula is necessary for the unity of the church. These doctrines are those "which always and everywhere were received in all the Churches of the Augsburg Confession." This reminds us of the rule of Vincent of Lerins in the fifth century, that what is catholic is that which is believed "always, everywhere, and by everyone" (*semper, ubique, et ab omnibus*). Within the Lutheran church, there is concern to receive the *magnam consensus*—the great consensus of the catholic tradition.

The Formula brought theological unity to the Lutheran church in the empire. It also excluded those followers of Melanchthon who were branded as "Crypto-Calvinists" and were driven into the German Reformed camp. That is the nature of confessions. They testify to "what we believe, teach, and confess." They exclude those who believe, teach, and confess something different. In the situation of state-supported churches, the confessions become legal documents, and subscription to them was often required for positions in the church, the civil realm, and the universities. (This was the case in the Reformed, Roman Catholic, and Anglican lands as well as Lutheran.) But in non-establishment situations, the confessions serve as witnesses to the gospel. They become acts of confessing the faith in situations where the faith is challenged.

The best example of confessional situations in modern times is the Barmen Declaration of the Confessing Church in Germany in 1934.[13] This statement of the Confessing Church, drafted principally by Karl Barth with in-put from other theologians such as Dietrich Bonhoeffer, opposed the Nazi-supported "German-Christian" national Church. It specifically rejected the subordination of the church to the state, declaring that the church "is solely Christ's property."

Also, in recent times, the Lutheran World Federation declared that apartheid in South Africa presented "a state of confession" (*status confessionis*); it could not be an "indifferent matter" (*adiaphoron*). The Lutheran confessional concern was not so much that some things are *adiaphora*, that is, matters that have no bearing on salvation (which may therefore be treated with indifference). Rather, sometimes, in a state of confession (*in statu confessionis*), some matters cannot be "indifferent."

Attitudes toward the Confessions

What identity do the confessions provide for contemporary Lutherans? Lutherans in America have had several different approaches to the confessions.[14] One approach, associated especially but not exclusively with The Lutheran Church–Missouri Synod, has held that we subscribe to the confessions "because" (*quia*) they are true. In matters upon which the confessions touch, we have a true and reliable interpretation of Scripture, and they can even shed light on matters they do not directly address. Those who subscribe to the confessions in this way insist that the Lutheran church should teach what the confessions teach and hold its teachers accountable to confessional teachings in their own teaching.

The other view, espoused especially by the nineteenth-century "American Lutheran" platform of Simon S. Schmucker, acknowledges developments since the sixteenth century but holds that the confessions are a part of our heritage. What is most important about the confessions is their witness to the unchanging gospel of Jesus Christ. So we subscribe to the confessions "in so far" (*quatenus*) as they are true interpretations of Scripture. The problem with this form of subscription, as Schmucker's critics pointed out, is that it really commits the subscriber to nothing specific. The confessions get treated on a case-by-case basis. Schmucker himself waffled on baptismal regeneration and the real presence of Christ in the Eucharist, in an effort to make common cause with American evangelicalism, which has had difficulty affirming the necessity of baptism as a means of grace (God's act, not a human decision) and the presence of the body and blood of Christ in, with, and under the bread and the wine.

A more "constructive" approach to the confessions takes seriously both the confessions and contemporary issues. The confessions give the church clarity in preaching the gospel of Christ; this is their evangelical thrust. But the confessions also root us in the Catholic tradition. They appeal to the authority of the church fathers and the norming authority of the Bible. This evangelical catholic approach to the confessions serves the purpose of shoring up Lutheran identity while also building ecumenical bridges to other Christian traditions that preach the same gospel and share in the same great tradition.

This appeal both to the gospel of justification by faith in God's saving work in Christ and to the great tradition paid off in 1999, when the Lutheran World Federation and the Roman Catholic Church signed the *Joint Declaration on the Doctrine of Justification*. The joint declaration does not say everything that Lutherans would want to say about justification, nor does it say everything Roman Catholics would want to say about sanctification. But it encompasses a core teaching that we are justified by faith in Christ and given the grace to accomplish the good works God wants us to perform. The core affirmation is this:

15. In faith we together hold the conviction that justification is the work of the triune God. The Father sent his Son into the world to save sinners. The foundation and presupposition of justification is the incarnation, death, and resurrection of Christ. Justification thus means that Christ himself is our righteousness, in which we share through the Holy Spirit in accord with the will of the Father. Together we confess: By grace alone, in faith in Christ's saving work and not because of any merit on our part, we are accepted by God and receive the Holy Spirit, who renews our hearts while equipping and calling us to good works.[15]

"The article on which the church stands or falls" has become the first great step toward healing the breach of the sixteenth century. A church that confesses that we are justified "by grace alone, in faith in Christ's saving work and not because of any merit on our part" is not a fallen church. And Lutherans, on their part, need to recognize that the work of the Holy Spirit in our lives should count for something in "calling us to good works."

Questions for Discussion

1. Can you envision the Augsburg Confession serving the cause of Christian unity? How?

2. How is the Lutheran distinction between law and gospel evident today in Lutheran preaching and pastoral care?

3. How does *The Small Catechism* function as lay theology?

4. What role do you see the confessions playing in Lutheran identity today?

5

Common Liturgy

The faith and life of the Christian community is expressed in public rites called "liturgy" (from the Greek word *leitourgia*, pertaining to "public work"). It is not surprising that, early on in the Reformation, liturgical reform became an urgent necessity. The Reformers understood the relationship between the "rule of prayer" (*lex orandi*) and the "rule of faith" (*lex credendi*). In other words, there is a correlation between prayer and belief, worship and doctrine, with primacy accruing to prayer and worship because these are experiential, whereas belief and doctrine are reflective. Martin Luther got into the act of liturgical reform because others were doing it—but not doing it well, in his estimation. He saw no need to throw out the historic liturgical rites of the church and start over. The historic liturgical rites had served the purpose of expressing the relationship between God and God's people very well for many centuries. The traditional rites simply needed to be corrected and purified. In particular, Luther applied his surgeon's knife to the Canon of the Mass (what we today call the Great Thanksgiving), because the Roman canon spoke of "our offerings and oblations" rather than the Christ's gift of Communion. Other than that, much of the rest of the Mass remained intact.

Luther wrote a treatise in 1523 titled *The Form of the Mass and Communion for the Church at Wittenberg,* which provided guidance in the reform of the Latin Mass and Communion practices. Germans had been used to singing vernacular songs within the Mass, and Luther called for the composition of additional vernacular songs that could be sung by evangelical congregations. In 1526 he prepared a treatise *The German Mass and Order of Service* that provided a kind of song mass for use in village churches that lacked trained choirs to sing the ordinary and propers of the Latin Mass. This song mass (*lied Messe*) established a set of chorale versifications or tropes on the "ordinary" parts of the Mass: the Kyrie, Gloria, Credo, Sanctus, and Agnus Dei. The chorales that became associated with these parts of the Mass include "Kyrie, God Father in Heaven Above," "All Glory Be to God on High," "We All Believe in One True God," "Isaiah, Mighty Seer in Days of Old," and "Lamb of God, Pure and Sinless" or "O Christ, Thou Lamb of God." These chorales have remained in Lutheran hymnals ever since.

Church Orders

Luther's liturgical writings carried no ecclesiastical or political authority. They were undoubtedly used as models, since aspects of his Latin and German masses remained in Lutheran practice for centuries, especially the music he provided for the German Mass. But officially instituting liturgical changes required official church orders or ordinances. This required getting the powers-that-be to adopt and implement officially the Reformation agenda. When the Reformation was adopted, it had to be put into law. Church ordinances were needed to regulate practice and liturgical use.

As the Reformation was adopted in cities and lands, it was implemented by law through church orders. Johannes Bugenhagen, Luther's colleague at Wittenberg, was kept busy drafting church orders across northern Germany and for the kingdom of Denmark. Johannes Brenz wrote church orders for south German territories.

Probably the most significant church order produced by Brenz, in collaboration with Andreas Osiander, the chief pastor and reformer of Nuremberg, was for Nuremberg in 1533. This order was also adopted by Margrave Joachim II of Brandenburg when he implemented the Reformation in his territory. The Brandenburg-Nuremburg Church Order provided for the Mass in both Latin and German. It proved to be influential not only in Germany but also in England. Thomas Cranmer, the future reforming archbishop of Canterbury, had been in Nuremberg as an ambassador of King Henry VIII to the imperial court when the evangelical Mass was implemented in 1533, and he had a copy of this church order in his library.

In these church orders, we see a mixture of Latin and German parts in a liturgical order that was roughly the same from one territory to another, and retained the basic shape of the historic liturgy of the Mass and the prayer offices of matins and vespers. The tendency was to "correct" the pre-Reformation liturgical books, which were in Latin, until these books were destroyed in the devastations of the Thirty Years' War and new books had to be printed. Nevertheless, Latin remained in use in several Lutheran cities, including Nuremberg and Leipzig, throughout the eighteenth century. In part, this was because choral settings of Latin texts had been composed for use with the evangelical mass.[1]

Luther's desire for more congregational song was met by composers and independent printers. (Unlike today, hymnals were not authorized; they were entrepreneurial enterprises.) Beginning with the *Eight Song Booklet* in 1524, hymnals began to appear. By the end of the century, Lutheran hymnals and choir books (*cantionales*) of gargantuan size were being published. People did not have these hymnals in pew racks. The choirs might have them, and people kept hymnals at home. But they had to memorize the hymns, and Luther and others often complained that the people weren't learning the songs fast enough.

Eventually, of course, Lutheran people did learn the songs, and an impressive repertoire was built up over several centuries of hymns that were known in various territories. Luther himself had composed about three-dozen hymns, and the composition of new hymns continued apace. The classic Reformation and post-Reformation hymns were also taken up by the great Lutheran composers and served as the basis of organ preludes and church cantatas, reaching a high point in the output of Johann Sebastian Bach. Lutherans coming to the New World brought their hymnals with them. Many eighteenth-century hymnals also included liturgical material. From the beginning, Lutheranism produced a singing church, and this has remained a characteristic of Lutheran identity up to the present and throughout the world.

Scandinavian Liturgies

The two types of Lutheran liturgy derived, respectively, from Luther's *Form of the Mass* and *German Mass* were transported to the

Scandinavian countries. Sweden's reformer Olavus Petri prepared a Swedish Mass in 1531 that was based on the model of Luther's *Form of the Mass* derived from the Rostock Hymnal. It includes a congregational confession of sins and a Communion service that includes the Words of Institution within an expanded eucharistic preface followed by the Sanctus ("Holy, holy, holy..."), Lord's Prayer, Pax ("The peace of the Lord..."), and a "Lamb of God" song. This vernacular mass was at first used only in Stockholm. Under Olavus's brother, Archbishop Laurentius Petri, the Swedish Mass was integrated with the Latin Mass through several revisions up through 1557, until the Swedish Church Order of 1571 provided a full Swedish High Mass. Even then, Latin was not entirely suppressed in the cathedrals because these churches had choirs to sing the old Latin settings. The same liturgy was used in the duchy of Finland until a Finnish Bible made possible a Finnish-language version of the Swedish Mass. Hymnody was not fully developed in Sweden until the early nineteenth century under Archbishop Johan Wallin (1779–1836).

Johannes Bugenhagen in 1537 helped prepare a Danish Church Order that includes an order of worship in Danish that was modeled on Luther's *German Mass*. Congregational song replaced the Latin choir chants, although, as in Sweden, the repertoire was limited at first. Whether a choral setting of Latin texts or a song setting of vernacular texts was used in Lutheran worship depended largely on the availability of resources such as Latin schools, whose boys' choirs were trained to sing Latin texts to plainsong or polyphonic settings.

Until vernacular Bibles were published, or at least a vernacular New Testament to provide the epistles and gospels for the Mass, evangelical vernacular worship was not possible. Luther's German New Testament was already published by the end of 1522, although Luther's complete German Bible wasn't ready in its definitive version until 1545. The strategy adopted by Luther and followed in other countries was to translate the Psalms and prophetic books first while working on the rest of the Old Testament, since these were also needed for liturgies (for example, introits and graduals, as well as psalmody and readings for matins and vespers). Olavus Petri produced a Swedish New Testament by 1526; a complete Swedish Bible (largely the work of Olavus Petri) was ready by 1541. The Finnish reformer Michael Agricola produced a Finnish New Testament in 1548, but a complete Finnish Bible wasn't published until 1642, due to restrictions placed on Finnish literature by the Swedish crown. A complete Danish Bible (King Christian III's Bible) was published in 1550. This Bible was also used in Norway until being replaced by King Frederick II's Bible in 1589. Norway did not receive its own church order until 1607. An Icelandic New Testament was prepared in 1540 by Oddur Gottsálksson; a complete Icelandic Bible was published in 1584 by Bishop Guðbrandur Thorláksson.

Hymnody developed profusely in Germany during the sixteenth and seventeenth centuries. Of these hymns, the chorales of Philipp Nicolai (1556–1608), specifically "Awake, Awake, for Night Is Flying" and "How Bright Shines the Morning Star," and the lyrics of Paul Gerhardt (1606–1676), set to tunes by Cantor Johann Crüger (1598-1662), in hymns such as "O Lord, How Shall I Meet You" and "Awake, My Heart, with Gladness," have pride of place. These lyrics and tunes have a warmth that was lacking in the older chorales and were sung as devotional pieces in the home before they acquired a place in public worship. A popular Danish hymnody also developed in the seventeenth century under Bishop Thomas Kingo (1634–1703). Iceland, which had produced the great medieval sagas, saw the composition of *Hymns of the Passion*, a collection of epic proportions by Hallgrímur Pétursson (1614–1674), after whom the great modern Hallgrims Church in Reykjavik is named. Hymnody with a folk character emerged in Scandinavia in the nineteenth century. Danish writer and bishop Nicolai N. S. Grundtvig (1783–1872) produced a wealth of lyrical hymns that were set to music with more of a folk quality than the old chorales. Examples include "Built on a Rock," "O Day Full of Grace," "The Bells of Christmas," and "Bright and Glorious Is the Sky," a favorite for the season of Epiphany. This hymnody spurred similar developments of spiritual folk songs in Norway, Sweden, and Finland, including "In Heaven Above," "Behold a Host," "With God as Our Friend," "Children of the Heavenly Father," "Arise, My Soul, Arise," and "Lost in the Night."

Muhlenberg's Liturgy

Lutheran immigrants to North America brought all of these traditions with them. Already upon his arrival in the British colonies in Pennsylvania in 1742, Henry Melchior Muhlenberg encountered Swedish and Finnish congregations along the Delaware River as well as Dutch congregations along the Hudson River and German settlers from many different German lands (there was no Germany as such before the German Empire in 1871). An issue that concerned Muhlenberg, a missionary pastor sent from Halle to minister to German congregations in Pennsylvania, still concerns Lutherans in America: What binds all these brothers and sisters in the faith together? His concern from the outset of his ministry was to bind them together into one church body for mutual support, and he used the liturgy as the tie that binds.

The liturgy that Muhlenberg had prepared was ratified as the authorized liturgy of the Ministerium of Pennsylvania at its first meeting on August 15, 1748.[2] The ministerium resolved to use this and no other liturgical forms in every congregation in the ministerium. Muhlenberg recognized that the Swedes would need their own liturgy because they worshiped in Swedish or, increasingly, in English (eventually becoming Episcopalian). Muhlenberg's Lutherans were culturally German. Realizing that he could not use the church order of any one church province in Germany, he turned to the liturgy that he had in hand, that of Saint Mary's Lutheran Church in London, which in turn had received it from the Lutheran Church in the Netherlands. He adapted it to the conditions of parish life in the New World, with its fewer resources of money and staff, so it followed the tradition of the German song mass. However, recognizing that occasional services might include English speakers as well as Germans, Muhlenberg took the orders for baptism and marriage from *The Book of Common Prayer* of the Church of England. This ecumenical gesture was also recognition that the Anglican and Lutheran churches were ecclesiastical cousins. In fact, the *summus episcopus* (supreme bishop) of Muhlenberg's home church in Electoral Hannover was also the "supreme head" of the Church of England, King George II.

This Liturgy of the Ministerium was circulated in handwritten copies and seems to have been followed by the pastors in the ministerium as faithfully as local conditions allowed.[3] It was a full Lutheran liturgy that compared favorably with the Common Service developed a century later. Congregations at first made use of whatever hymnals the German settlers had brought with them, and Muhlenberg directed the pastors to use the collects, epistles, and gospels printed in these. The most common hymnal in use in the British North American colonies was the Marburg Hymnal, and in 1762 Christopher Sauer of Germantown printed a copy that included the proper collects and readings. In 1786 the liturgy and hymnal were finally printed together, with very few revisions, because of the possibilities of union with the newly formed Episcopal Church in New York and the German Reformed Church in Pennsylvania. These consolidations never occurred, but this liturgy was used for forty years and was received by newly formed synods.[4]

The Common Service

Immigration from Germany and Scandinavia brought millions of Lutherans to North America in the nineteenth and early twentieth centuries. These newcomers swamped the Lutherans who had been in America since colonial times. Lutheran congregations organized into synods that reflected primarily ethnic heritage, and these synods produced hymnals and worship books in their members' language of origin. Even in Pennsylvania, the number of new arrivals kept the German language in use, and Gettysburg Seminary was barely able to provide sufficient pastors who were fluent in German to serve German-speaking congregations. Nevertheless, especially on the East Coast, there were Lutheran congregations that desired to hold worship in English. Providing a suitable English-language Lutheran liturgy became an urgent need in the decades after the Civil War.

In the 1880s, the General Council, General Synod, and United Synod of the South jointly authorized work to be done on a common service in the English language. Scholar-pastors of uncommon ability were enlisted in this work, including Edward T. Horn from the United

Synod of the South, George U. Wenner of the General Synod, and Beale Melanchthon Schmucker of the General Council. The principle under which the committee worked was that the Common Service should reflect "the common consent of the pure Lutheran liturgies of the sixteenth century, and when there is not an entire agreement among them the consent of the largest number of greatest weight." This rule left the door open to a fair amount of subjective assessment, and once the Common Service was published, it drew criticism, especially in the General Synod. Professor James Richards of Gettysburg Seminary questioned whether the rule had been followed in every instance, whether it was even possible to follow such a rule, and whether therefore the Common Service should be imposed on congregations. The criticism was ably answered not only by Horn and Wenner (Schmucker had died of a heart attack while trying to catch a train to deliver the manuscript to the printer), but also by such esteemed theologians at the Philadelphia Seminary as Charles Porterfield Krauth and Henry Eyster Jacobs.

One objection that Jacobs especially answered with a strong argument was that the drafters of the Common Service drew texts from *The Book of Common Prayer*. Jacobs argued that the prayer book was a Reformation liturgical book. Its first edition in 1549 was heavily influenced by Lutheran church orders, and now that Lutherans were ready to pray in English, they could borrow back the prayer book's texts.

The Common Service proved very popular with congregations that were recovering their Lutheran heritage after it had been lost in the Age of Rationalism. The service was included in the hymnals of one Lutheran church body after another. However, synods whose congregations worshiped primarily in a language other than English were slow to adopt the Common Service. Some of these synods (for example, Augustana) often used translations of their other rites (Swedish) for their English-language liturgy. But already in 1893, the English Synod of Missouri and Adjacent States adopted the Common Service and brought it into its 1911 merger with the Missouri Synod, in which it continued as the English District of the Missouri Synod. *The Lutheran Hymnal* of the Synodical Conference (1941) adopted a form of the Common Service.

The use of a common liturgy and hymnal also contributed to organic Lutheran unity. The *Common Service Book* (1917) preceded the formation of the United Lutheran Church in American in 1918 by merger of the General Council, the General Synod, and the United Synod of the South. Further joint liturgical work commenced after World War II, producing the *Service Book and Hymnal of the Lutheran Church in America* (1958), a book that built on the Common Service but opened up Lutheran worship to more ancient and ecumenical practices. This book preceded the formation of the American Lutheran Church in 1960 and the Lutheran Church in America in 1962. Further joint liturgical work commenced in 1966, after The Lutheran Church–Missouri Synod invited other Lutheran bodies to form an Inter-Lutheran Commission on Worship. The *Lutheran Book of Worship* (1978) again built on the Common Service. It also reflected the agenda of the modern liturgical renewal movements, to renew liturgy precisely as a corporate and public act, in its division of liturgical leadership roles and use of current English and musical styles. Lay "assisting ministers" (A) were assigned leadership roles in the liturgy that historically were taken by deacons (for example, singing litanies, reading lessons, leading the intercessory prayers, serving the cup during communion). Roles appropriate for ordained ministers were designated for the "presiding minister" (P). The speech of prayers tended to be indicative rather than subjunctive. Through-composed musical settings of the liturgy were offered in place of historic chants. This book preceded the formation of the Evangelical Lutheran Church in Canada in 1986 and the Evangelical Lutheran Church in America (ELCA) in 1988. Even though The Lutheran Church–Missouri Synod (LCMS) finally rejected the *Lutheran Book of Worship,* slightly revised *LBW* liturgies were included in the Missouri Synod's *Lutheran Worship* (1982). Thus, it would seem that liturgy has indeed been a common tie for Lutherans in North America. With the *Lutheran Book of Worship,* Muhlenberg's vision of "one book, one church" was close to realization.

Loosening Liturgical Ties

There has always been variation in liturgical practice from one congregation to another, even when a common worship book was used.

Indeed, local use characterizes the history of Christian liturgy. But local variations have usually fit within a common order and core material. The new development in the 1980s was that Lutheran congregations (like many other mainline and evangelical Protestant congregations) began to discard the use of a book entirely. The common order was abandoned in favor of seeker services that would attract and hold the unchurched. This has been the case in the LCMS as much as, if not more than, in the ELCA. This trend has involved buying into (literally) the approach used by successful megachurches and the principles of church growth and patterns of worship that come out of the evangelical revival tradition.

Since the mid-1990s, the seeker service approach has evolved into the "praise and worship" format that is promoted by neo-Pentecostal groups such as the Vineyard. Many congregations now offer so-called contemporary services as well as traditional services (which breaks up the congregation) or blended services (which often leave no one satisfied). Often these contemporary services are offered with the presupposition that the youth are attracted to them. But young adults today can be just as much attracted to traditional liturgies if they discern in the congregation's practices something authentic—and if the liturgies are characterized by quality music and preaching.

A principal argument in favor of the use of the historic liturgy is that it is biblical. As I said in chapter two, this does not mean that its order can be found in the Bible; rather, the words of the Bible pervade this form of worship. To use these historic orders is to be steeped in the Scriptures. Another argument in favor of the use of the historic liturgy is that it is Trinitarian. It is addressed to God the Father, Son, and Holy Spirit. And the content of the historic liturgy is Christ, "the lamb of God who takes away the sins of the world." Worship of the Trinity constitutes true orthodoxy since "orthodoxy" literally means "right praise" as much as "right teaching." Indeed, since prayer establishes belief, the prayer and praise must be right if the belief is to be right.[5]

In 2006 the two main Lutheran denominations in America produced new worship books: *Evangelical Lutheran Worship* (ELCA) and *Lutheran Service Book* (LCMS). Apart from the merits or demerits of these new worship resources, they still retain liturgical orders and music from the *Lutheran Book of Worship* that the ELCA and LCMS will continue to share in common. But these books part company with each other in that *Evangelical Lutheran Worship* avoids the use of the third person singular male pronoun for God in its version of the psalms and canticles and avoids the name "Father" wherever possible, whereas *Lutheran Service Book* ignores inclusive language almost entirely, including language referring to the human community. It would seem on the basis of historical example that Lutheran identity in worship calls for biblical translations that are faithful to the text, on the one hand, and use words that in today's currency intentionally comprehend the whole people, on the other. In the first instance the reformers distinguished between translations and paraphrases; in the second instance the reformers changed the pronouns of some prayers from singular to plural to include the whole congregation.

Liturgical Piety

The center of Lutheran church life and personal piety has been assembly around the preaching of the word of God and the administration of the sacraments of Christ. This has required training preachers and pastors to exercise the ministry of word and sacrament in the tradition of the Reformation and preparing the people to hear the word and inwardly digest it and to receive in faith the sacraments of Baptism and Holy Communion. The use of the catechism and individual confession and absolution has been important in preparing the people to receive the sacraments.

Since piety involves outward expressions of devotion, ritual actions are often employed. Ritual involves the use of the body, especially in the postures used in worship. Worshipers have sat for the epistle but stood for the gospel. They knelt to make confession and receive communion but stood for praise and thanksgiving. They bowed their head at the name of Jesus, traced the sign of the cross on their bodies at invocations of the Holy Trinity and benedictions, and folded their hands for prayer. These are devotional uses of the body that may be commended to us today.

The ambience of Lutheran church buildings did not change much from the Middle Ages into the Reformation era. There was no radical iconoclasm in Lutheran territories, especially after the iconoclastic campaign conducted in Wittenberg by Andreas Karlstadt during the time Luther was sequestered for safekeeping in Wartburg. Stained glass, statues, and pictures remained intact. Altars continued to be adorned with crucifixes, candles, and linens. These appointments were expressions of piety because they were paid for by the laity, who continued to provide bequests to their parish church in their wills as they had done in the pre-Reformation church. The witness of our liturgical spaces should continue to summon our attention today.

Many customs of the church year continued to be observed in the churches and in the homes of Christians. To be sure, the blessing of wine on Saint John's Day, candles on Candlemas, ashes on Ash Wednesday, and palms on Palm Sunday were abolished during the Reformation because of superstitious uses of these blessed objects. Four centuries later, it has been found beneficial to restore these blessings and use of candles, ashes, and palms. The candles and palms can be taken home as reminders of the light of Christ coming into the world and in anticipation of his coming again. Advent wreaths were practically invented by Lutherans and were used in the home long before they acquired a place in the church buildings. Lutherans also made use of the Christmas tree in the home and in the church building. Lutherans observed fast days, especially during Lent, and also feast days, especially Christmas and Easter. The distinction between times of fasting and feasting, and proper ways of practicing fasts and feasts, would be salutary ways of enabling Christians to identify with the passion and glorification of Christ in their everyday lives.

During the Reformation, Lutherans continued to observe some saints' days, although many were abolished in order to reduce the number of days each year not given to productive labor. The days of the apostles, the evangelists, such pre-Reformation Marian festivals as the Annunciation, the Visitation, and the Purification of Mary and Presentation of Jesus, as well as the Nativity of Saint John the Baptist and Saint Michael and All Angels remained on Lutheran calendars.

Some church orders also provided for the commemorations of Mary Magdalene, Lawrence, Francis of Assisi, Elizabeth of Thuringia, and Bernard of Clairvaux. Since 1978 the calendar of commemorations for Lutherans has been greatly expanded in the *Lutheran Book of Worship*. The observance of these saints' days is a way of maintaining the bond between the church militant (the church on earth) and the church triumphant (the church in heaven), which is also celebrated in Christian funerals. Lutherans do not pray to the saints or to the faithful departed, but Melanchthon grants in *The Apology*, "The saints in heaven pray for the church in general, as they prayed for the church universal while they were on earth" (article 21).[6] *The Apology* testifies that we give honor to the saints, first, to thank God for showing mercy by revealing his will to save and to give gifts to the church; second, because the examples of the saints strengthen our faith; and third, because the saints serve as models for us in our Christian callings.

The daily prayer offices remained in many Lutheran churches during and after the Reformation era, especially where adjoining Latin schools provided boys' choirs to sing the psalms and canticles (as in the case of Saint Thomas School and Church in Leipzig). Particular emphasis was given to Saturday Vespers, which included confession and absolution before receiving Communion on Sunday, the ancient station days of Wednesday and Friday on which the Great Litany was prayed, and the eves of great festivals such as Christmas and Pentecost, for which there was often a choral evensong. The prayer offices relate to the natural rhythms of darkness and light, of night and day, of rest and work, which possess profound symbolic power. Not every Christian is able to attend public daily morning prayer and evening prayer, but matins and vespers should be offered in our churches for those who are able to attend, and the laity should be trained to pray morning and evening prayer at home, using brief forms with essential elements of the office or the catechism.

Hymn singing became an important part of Lutheran piety by the end of the sixteenth century. Not only did the people learn and sing hymns in church, they also sang hymns at home. Some well-known Lutheran hymns developed out of household devotions before becoming corporate songs of the church. An example is Martin Rinkart's "Now Thank We All Our God," which was written during a time of plague as a thanksgiving for deliverance and was probably sung at table. It has become known as the Lutheran Te Deum. Lutherans purchased their own hymnals; before the nineteenth century, hymnals were not provided in churches. It has been a custom in many congregations to give hymnals to confirmands. Whether or not the youth actually use their hymnals, the custom should be continued because this is a profoundly symbolic way to reinforce the connection between home and church. (Sometimes the books are consulted and used!)

Liturgical piety pertains to devotions at home as well as to liturgy in the assembly. Luther's Small Catechism enjoins on Christians the daily recitation of the Apostles' Creed and the Lord's Prayer. The creed reminds us of the Trinitarian structure of the Christian worldview, and the seven petitions of the Lord's Prayer comprehend everything that we should ask of the Lord in prayer. Trinitarian liturgical formularies such as invocations and the Gloria Patri are used at home as well as in church, as Luther indicates in the morning and evening prayers in his Small Catechism. Table graces in the Catechism become an amplification of the fourth petition of the Lord's Prayer, which Luther explains as including "everything required to satisfy our bodily needs, such as food and clothing, house and home, fields and flocks, money and property; a pious spouse and good children, trustworthy servants, godly and faithful rulers, good government; seasonable weather, peace and health, order and honor; true friends, faithful neighbors, and the like."[7] Our piety even at the family table reminds us of our relationship to the Creator and to the whole of creation, including the neighbor whose needs are identified in the explanations to the Ten Commandments in Luther's Catechisms. One aspect of Lutheran piety is service to the neighbor in need. We shall take up this part of piety in the concluding chapter.

Questions for Discussion

1. How are Luther's two liturgical models—Latin Mass and German Mass—replicated in liturgical styles in Lutheran congregations today?

2. What resources were needed for a full evangelical catholic liturgy at the time of the Reformation? What resources are needed for worship today?

3. How easy or difficult was it to teach people new ways of worship at the time of the Reformation? How easy or difficult is liturgical change today? Why?

4. In what ways can there be a correlation between worship in the church and devotions at home?

6

Witness in Society

There is a common stereotype that the Protestant Reformers of the sixteenth century separated public and private morality and were indifferent to the ethical importance of social structures and institutions. In *Beyond Charity*, Carter Lindberg calls this understanding into question.[1] He shows how the Reformers reacted to the medieval point of view that was formed by the piety of achievement, or what the Reformers called "works righteousness." One did a good work to merit grace. Medieval piety idealized poverty, either as a voluntary renunciation of wealth by entering monasteries and convents (a good work on the part of monks and nuns) or as a way of providing for the Christian duty of almsgiving (a good work done by the almsgiver). In either case, the material effects on actual poverty were slight, and the religious endorsement of poverty precluded urban efforts to address the growing problem of the poor created by the number of peasants making their way into the towns and cities, looking for better employment opportunities. The Reformers, impelled by their theology, developed new structures for addressing social welfare needs. Martin Luther may have been one of the first persons in modern history to propose a community chest to take care of the basic needs of the urban poor and to curtail begging, including the begging of the mendicant monks that Luther himself had once done.

Lindberg shows that the key to the Reformers' undertakings was the conviction that social ethics is the continuation of community worship. Luther defined *Gottesdienst* (service of God) as both worship and community service. The community chest was maintained by almsgiving in the churches. A custom that emerged in Lutheran and Anglican churches was that communicants would deposit alms in the collection for the poor as they made their way into the chancel to receive the sacrament. Thus, a connection was made between being fed at God's table and feeding the hungry and clothing the naked.

This collection was not for the maintenance of churches. That was taken care of by church taxes and by provisions in wills. Many items were provided for divine services in the wills of parishioners, who on their deathbed also usually left something for the poor of the parish.[2] Since Lutheran churches did not engage in iconoclasm, as the Reformed and Anglicans did, it was still possible to provide the parish church with candlesticks, crucifixes, pictures, and vestments. But all the Reformers encouraged provision for the poor in last wills and testaments, as well as charity for the needy neighbor in one's daily life as a Christian—no longer as a way of meriting grace at the last minute, as in late medieval piety, but as a final thankful response to God's unmerited grace already freely given and received in faith.

Marriage and Family

There is probably no area in which the Reformation exerted a greater impact on society than in marriage and family life. The reform of marriage began with recognition of the need to reform convents and monasteries. Many noble families had placed their unmarried daughters and non-inheriting sons in cloisters. There's no doubt that some men and women of both noble and humble backgrounds rose to positions of prominence in monastic orders. But many were placed in cloisters against their wills. Escaping from cloisters was not easy, and many women who resisted their vows were bullied and punished by superiors.

Luther, in the meantime, was coming to a new appreciation of marriage as a divine institution. As a biblical scholar, he saw marriage at the beginning and end of the Bible (Genesis 2:18-25; Revelation 19:9) and as a metaphor for the relationship between Israel and God (Hosea 6:7-11) and between Christ and the church (Ephesians 5:21-33). Marriage is a good estate intended by God for all human beings except those who are voluntarily celibate for the sake of the kingdom. Luther insisted that fathers have a responsibility to arrange proper marriages for all their children.[3] He even actively encouraged fathers to remove their daughters from convents, by force if necessary. In 1523 he approved the example of the Torgau burgher Leonhard Koppe, who successfully plotted the escape of his daughter and eleven nuns from the convent at Nimbschen. One of these nuns was Katherine von Bora, whom Luther married in 1525 after helping to arrange matches for the other escaped nuns.

As far as Luther was concerned, opportunities for marriage abounded, and he considered women well endowed by their Creator to be wives and mothers. The Reformers all rejected the ascetic sexuality of Jerome, Augustine, and other church fathers, as well as the medieval view that marriage was given to human beings only to enable them to avoid the sin of concupiscence and to populate the earth. For Lutherans, a satisfying sexual relationship between husband and wife was considered essential to a good marriage. The reformers sanctioned divorce and remarriage on the grounds of adultery, willful abandonment, chronic impotence, life-threatening hostility, and willful deceit (as when a bride considered to have been a virgin before marriage gives birth to an illegitimate child or is impregnated by another man).[4] Luther also objected to the many impediments to marriage enshrined in canon law, such as the need to get a dispensation to marry within the bloodline even down to the third cousin and the ban on marriages within spiritual affinities, such as between godparents and godchildren.

The medieval church had approved the secret marriages of youth (boys as early as fourteen, girls as early as twelve) without their parents' approval. Luther felt that this represented a cavalier approach to a divine institution and did not augur well for good and lasting marriages. He felt that youth should have their parents' blessing before marrying, but also that parents should not push their children into a marriage the children don't want. The title of a tract on the subject says it all: *Parents Should Neither Compel nor Hinder the Marriage of Their Children and Children Should Not Marry without the Consent of Their Parents.*

It was precisely to avoid secret marriage that Luther promoted public rites of marriage. Even though he regarded marriage as an institution that should be regulated by the civil authorities, since it is not a sacrament of the church but available to all people, he nevertheless encouraged marriages to be solemnized at the church building, with the banns or announcement of the impending marriage to be read to the congregation on three successive Sundays, the betrothal to take place on the church porch (as in the medieval rite), and a procession to the altar for the word of God and blessing.[5] The nuptial mass was no longer celebrated because it fell into the category of a votive mass. But in Strasbourg, Martin Bucer recommended that weddings take place on Sundays at the Communion service, so that the first act of married life would be receiving the Sacrament of the Altar with the congregation. Weddings often took place on a Sunday because this was also a day off from work for ordinary people.

As the early Lutheran clergy stumbled over one another in their rush to get married, they also took seriously the role of the parsonage family as a model Christian family to be emulated by the laity. Luther became not only a theologian, reformer, and pastor, but also a husband and father of six children. In his own marriage and family life, we might regard him as quite enlightened for his age. He had a high regard for Katy's business and managerial skills, and his discipline of his children avoided corporal punishment (something he had experienced as a boy). Katherine Luther ran a large household in a large house—the former Black Cloister of the Augustinians that the elector of Saxony gave to the Luthers as a wedding gift. Within this house, she boarded a number of students, often entertained many guests at the family table (the source of Luther's "Table Talk," in which his discussions during meals were recorded by students), and operated a successful beer-making business. In his will, Luther left his whole estate to his wife, which was an uncommon gesture at the time.

In Lutheranism marriage became less a social contract and more a covenant of love and faithfulness between husband and wife. Sex, marriage, and family moved out of the realm of canon law and into the practice of pastoral care. While Lutheranism has recognized civil society's vested interest in these matters, it has continued to see the need to place all of the orders of creation—including family and state—under the word of God.

Lutheran Charitable and Educational Institutions

What became of the monasteries in the territories that implemented the Reformation? Lutheran regimes were not as ruthless in dismantling the cloisters as King Henry VIII of England and the Reformed churches were. Nevertheless, monks and nuns were encouraged to leave the cloisters and find vocations in the world. Those who clung to the old faith were subjected to Lutheran sermons in their chapels; the nuns in the famous Vadstena Cloister in Sweden silently protested Lutheran sermons by stuffing wax in their ears. Monks and nuns who were aged or ill were allowed to stay or were pensioned off to be cared for elsewhere. The empty monasteries were turned into hospitals or schools, with some of the former nuns and monks serving as nurses and teachers in these new evangelical institutions.

Charitable and educational institutions have been an important feature of Lutheran identity throughout the centuries. In this section, we will look at several examples of Lutheran pioneers in education, social services, and the mission of the gospel at home and abroad.

August Hermann Francke (1663–1727) is one of the most interesting figures in Lutheran history. He was strongly influenced by Pietism, which Philip Jacob Spener (1635–1705) defined as a movement to "convert the outward orthodox profession into a living theology of the heart." Spener sought to do this by means of practical programs that included public Bible study and private Bible reading, a revival of Luther's concept of "the priesthood of all believers" by engaging lay Christians in practical acts of love and service to the neighbor, ending unnecessary theological controversies (especially in the pulpit), reforming theological education to stress spiritual formation as much as academic study, and gathering Christians into small groups (conventicles) called *collegia pietatis* for mutual support in growth in holiness (sanctification).[6]

Francke studied ancient Hebrew and classical Greek at the universities of Erfurt and Kiel. After a conversion experience in 1685, which resolved his doubts about the Lutheran confessions and the word of God, he enrolled at the University of Hamburg to study the Bible with Johann Winkler, an ardent disciple of Spener. He went through a series of academic and pastoral positions in orthodox Leipzig and Saxony, from all of which he was dismissed because of his promotion of conventicles, which the authorities regarded as subversive and a cause of religious and political dissension. In 1691 he went to stay with Spener in Berlin for two months and to rehabilitate his reputation as a scholar and pastor. There he came to the attention of the elector of Brandenburg, Frederick William, who was promoting Pietism as an irenic form of practical Christianity that would transcend the polemics of the orthodox Lutherans and Reformed in the expanding Hohenzollern territories. Francke was called as pastor of Saint George Church and professor of classical Greek and Hebrew at the new University of Halle, both of which were endowed by the elector, in 1691. In 1713 the new elector and king of Prussia, Frederick William I, visited Halle and gave public support to Francke, who the next year was called as pastor of the main city church of Saint Ulrich.

From this position, Francke began to collect alms that led to the establishment of various educational and charitable institutions. The first was a school for poor orphaned children. With more funds, it became a boarding school. With still more funds, Francke bought the large house next to the parsonage and turned it into an orphanage. Other institutions followed: a system of "German schools" (as an alternative to the traditional Latin schools) for children from every walk of life, a teacher's training school, and a Bible institute that published biblical literature. The students at the schools received excellent medical care and free lunches. Under Francke's leadership, the university became a training center not only for pastors but also for missionaries to be sent to other parts of the world. Henry Melchior Muhlenberg (1711–1787) later came to Halle to be trained as a missionary to India, but instead he was persuaded by Francke's son, Gotthilf August, to go to Pennsylvania as the pastor to the Lutheran settlers there. Johann Freylinghausen (1670–1739), Francke's son-in-law, published the great pietist hymnal out of the Halle Orphanage; it sold thousands of copies and was brought by Lutheran immigrants to the British North American colonies. The German schools became the nucleus of free and compulsory elementary education in the kingdom of Prussia, later studied by the American educator Horace Mann.[7]

The expanding kingdom of Prussia and the expanding hegemony of the House of Hollenzollern in Germany, who were of the Reformed confession, created a serious confessional problem for Lutherans in the nineteenth century. King Frederick William III proposed a union of the Lutheran and Reformed churches with himself as highest bishop (*summus episcopus*) in 1817, the three hundredth anniversary of Luther's Ninety-Five Theses. This "Prussian Union" was enforced through strict measures and was being emulated even in territories with Lutheran rulers. Some Lutherans found it necessary to emigrate. (They included the Saxons who settled in the Mississippi Valley and formed The Lutheran Church–Missouri Synod in 1847 and those who moved to Australia in the same time period and settled in and around Adelaide.) The Lutheran resistance proved so strong that the king finally allowed an Evangelical Lutheran Church in Prussia to be formed in 1841. This struggle for Lutheran identity produced a confessional revival throughout Germany that was carried by emigrants to North America, Australia, and South Africa. In 1830 the tercentenary of the Augsburg Confession August F. C. Vilmar (1800–1868), later a professor of theology at Marburg, called for the renewal of the church based on a strict confessionalism. Many pastors and theologians responded to this call.

One was Wilhelm Löhe (1808–1872), the pastor in the Bavarian village of Neuendettelsau. In this small community, Löhe developed a renewed liturgy based on the church orders of the sixteenth century, moved toward the realization of word and sacrament every Lord's Day and festival, and retrieved the practice of individual confession and absolution. He established a deaconess motherhouse, which had affiliated hospitals, orphanages, homes for the elderly, and educational institutions. For the devotional life of the deaconess community, he restored the daily prayer offices of the church. He also established a mission society with links to North America, South America, and Australia. Pastors trained in the mission institute in Neuendettelsau served congregations in Ohio, Michigan, and Iowa, whose synods later formed the American Lutheran Church (1930), a distant predecessor body of the Evangelical Lutheran Church in America.

In Scandinavia, Lutheranism received a reawakening that was as much influenced by Pietism as by German Neo-Lutheranism. But the influence of the leading revivalists on society was profound. In Denmark, Nicolai F. S. Grundtvig (1783–1872), a leading educator, poet, and theologian in his country, established folk schools that aligned Lutheranism with the folk culture of the people. In Norway, Hans Nielsen Hauge (1771–1824), a businessman and lay preacher who was frequently arrested for street preaching and organizing conventicles, nevertheless remained loyal to the state church and infused a new spirit in the official Lutheranism of his country. In Sweden, Pastor Lars Laestadius (1800–1861) and lay preacher Carl Olof Rosenius (1816–1868) created a revival within the state Lutheran church, calling for moral regeneration at home and mission abroad. In Finland, the preaching of the farmer Paavo Ruotsalainen (1777–1852), calling for repentance and the need for intense prayer, found many sympathetic ears among lay people and clergy. Pastors influenced by Ruotsalainen used individual confession as a means to bring about repentance. The felt need for a spiritual awakening in Finland became acute when the land passed from Swedish to Russian rule in 1809, and it played a role in the Finnish struggle for independence.

Back in Germany, the continuing concern for practical Christianity produced a movement that emphasized "home mission" or "inner mission" as well as foreign mission. Alsatian pastor John F. Oberlin (1740–1826) advocated social justice by creating schools, savings banks, and agricultural societies. Pastor John Falk (1768–1828) created foster homes and "recovery houses" for impoverished youth who had gotten in trouble with the authorities. Pastor Theodore Fliedner (1800–1864) of Kaiserswerth in the lower Rhineland advocated antipoverty programs, prison reform, and a more equal role for women in the new industrial society. He established the first deaconess motherhouse and a training center for women involved in church work. The most effective spokesman of the inner mission movement in Germany was Pastor Johann H. Wichern (1808–1881), who called attention to the social problems of children and youth in the new industrial society and established an educational center for juvenile delinquents known as "rough house"

(*Rauhes Haus*).[8] By the 1840s, inner mission societies were spring-ing up throughout Germany and were spreading to Scandinavia and America. This inner mission work was spearheaded in the United States by William A. Passavant (1821–1894), the pastor of First Lutheran Church in Pittsburgh and a founder of the Pittsburgh Synod, who was inspired by the work of Thedore Fliedner. Passavant brought several deaconess sisters from Kaiserswerth to Pittsburgh, where in 1849 he founded the first Protestant hospital and orphanage in the United States. Under Passavant's influence, Lutheran hospitals were established in Milwaukee, Chicago, and Jacksonville, Illinois, and orphanages were established at Mount Vernon, New York; Germantown, Pennsylvania; and Boston, Massachusetts. The indefatigable Passavant, through his editorials in his publication *The Missionary*, expanded inner mission work to embrace concern not only for social victims but for all work of the church, including education and architecture.

Lutheranism has shown a concern to meet the needs of those members of the human family who fall through the cracks of the social structure, especially orphans and widows, the hungry and the destitute, and refugees from political catastrophe and natural disaster. Lutheran people have met these needs through social agencies and relief organi-zations, through world hunger appeals and local hands-on ministries. This has been a Lutheran strength. These ministries have provided means whereby the faithful show their faith active in deeds of love.

Art and Music

Lutheranism has made a significant contribution to Western cul-ture in the areas of art and music. After the experience of Karlstadt's iconoclasm in Wittenberg in 1522, Luther resisted all efforts to remove artwork from the churches. Such "outward things," he said, will "not harm a person's faith, as long as the heart does not cleave to them or put its trust in them."[9] In and of themselves, images are neither good nor evil; they are *adiaphora*—"indifferent matters." As long as they are not used superstitiously, Lutheran theologians held that they serve a useful purpose as "books of the laity" and "Scripture for the poor."[10] There was no wholesale destruction of altarpieces or stained-glass windows in churches that became Lutheran once Luther ran Karlstadt out of town.

In fact, there was even an increase in new works of art commissioned for churches under Lutheran patronage. Art historians have suggested that more new altarpieces were installed in northern Germany, where the Cranachs were considered the orthodox Lutheran painters, than in the parts of Germany that remained loyal to the old faith. Most of the main churches in Saxony and Brandenburg were decorated with the artwork of Lucas Cranach the Elder (1472–1553) and his son Lucas Cranach the Younger (1515–1586).

Cranach the Elder was a close friend of Luther. They were godfathers to one another's children and collaborated in producing woodcuts and book illustrations that helped spread the views of the Reformation in its early years. The elder Cranach also served as court artist to the electors of Saxony Frederick the Wise, John the Steadfast, and John Frederick the Magnanimous. In Wittenberg he maintained a large and productive workshop that prepared paintings for the churches of Saxony as well as the electoral residences.

The son continued his father's work and served as burgomaster of Wittenberg from 1565 to 1568. Among his famous paintings are *Allegory of Law and Grace* for the Collegiate Church at Weimar. The three huge panels included portraits of Martin Luther, Lucas Cranach the Elder, and Elector John Frederick with his family. His *Last Supper* shows Luther and other Reformers in the guise of disciples of Jesus at the Last Supper. Frequent use of the eucharistic theme distinguished the paintings of the Cranachs from the works of their medieval predecessors. This theme became all the more noteworthy in the works of Cranach the Younger in view of the "contentious climate" of "the new prominence given to eucharistic theology by the debates of the Reformation."[11] The work of the Cranachs was outspokenly Lutheran. Significantly, the influx of Calvinist ideas during the brief electorate of Christian I hastened the decline of the Cranach workshop because (a) commissions for new liturgical art dried up and (b) existing art was removed from the church buildings. In 1615 Margrave Johann Georg of Brandenburg had all the Cranach art work removed from the Berlin Cathedral and placed in the private palace chapel where his wife, the Electress Anna, had Lutheran services conducted.

Even more than in the arts of worship, Lutheranism has made a tremendous contribution to church music. Luther's German Mass made hymns an essential part of the Mass. He encouraged poets and composers by writing thirty-six hymns himself. The melodies for these hymns did not come from the beer halls, as the myth has it, but from the Gregorian chant and Meistersinger tradition of German art songs. Luther also endorsed a continuation and expansion of choral (choir) music, both Gregorian chant and the polyphonic motet. Luther made very few pronouncements on the use of the organ. He didn't think it was needed for the Mass, but that was because Gregorian chant was unaccompanied. By the end of the sixteenth century, however, the organ was being used to introduce congregational hymns and was alternating stanzas of the chorales with the congregation and the choir.

By the end of the sixteenth century, there were also complaints that the organ and Latin choral music and other parts in the service for the choir were depriving the congregation of their singing role and diminishing the spoken word.[12] Friedrich Blume writes, "Even those parts of the Mass rejected by Lutheran doctrine . . . , the Offertory and Communion [verses], forced their way into the service in the guise of the Latin motet." Congregational singing declined, and the service ceased to be understood by common people who didn't know Latin. The Latin choral music appealed to the intellectual elite. Blume argued that this situation "offered Calvinism the broadest field of attack."[13] But this point is debatable since the more elaborate services were held in electoral Brandenburg where the common people offered the greatest resistance to the Calvinism of their rulers.[14]

Nevertheless, choral and organ music flourished in the Lutheran church for the next two hundred years. Among scores of competent Lutheran composers, we may note the following who have gained broad public recognition in recent years through concerts and recordings: Michael Praetorius (1560–1629) of Hamburg; Heinrich Schütz (1585–1672) of Dresden, probably the greatest German composer of the seventeenth century; Johann Pachelbel (1653–1706) of Nuremberg; Georg Phillipp Telemann (1681–1767), who turned down the post of cantor at the Thomaskirche in Leipzig in 1721 to accept the position of cantor of the Johanneum (St. John Church and School) and music director of Hamburg.

The second choice of the search committee for the vacant cantorship of the Thomaskirche in Leipzig was Johann Sebastian Bach (1685–1750). He left the Calvinist court of Anhalt-Cöthen, where he composed many of his orchestral works, for the Leipzig post, in order to return to composing Lutheran church music and to secure better educational advantages for his sons. From Bach's days in Leipzig (1723–1750), where he also served as music director of the city and its churches, we have several hundred cantatas, six unaccompanied motets, chorale preludes, the *Saint Matthew Passion* and *Saint John Passion*, a Christmas oratorio comprising six cantatas for the Christmas season, the Magnificat in D, several Lutheran masses, and the great Mass in B Minor.

It is often said that Bach was neglected after his death. It's true that the music style changed in the mid-eighteenth century. Bach's sons—Wilhelm Friedemann (1710–1784), organist in Dresden and then in Halle; Karl Phillip Emanuel (1714–1788), a musician at the court of Frederick the Great and then Telemann's successor at Hamburg (he failed to receive the appointment as his father's successor at Leipzig); and Johann Christian (1735–1782), the so-called "London Bach," who converted to Roman Catholicism and served as organist at the Milan Cathedral before moving to London—took up the new rococo style. Bach's contemporary, a Lutheran from Halle, George Frederick Handel (1685–1759), also thrived in England, where his more homophonic style was preferred to strict counterpoint, but principally as a composer of operas, oratorios, and some anthems for the Anglican Church. Nevertheless, the elder Bach's scores were studied by Mozart and Beethoven. Bach's works were championed by such Romantic composers as Robert Schumann and Felix Mendelssohn-Barthody. Mendelssohn's concert performance of the *Saint Matthew Passion* on March 11, 1829, a hundred years after its first performance, is one of the most celebrated revivals in music history and launched a century and a half of Bach revival with the establishment of numerous Bach societies in Germany and America. Today Bach's church cantatas are performed in their liturgical setting in many churches in Germany and America.

Felix Mendelssohn (1809–1847) also should be mentioned as a contributor to Lutheran church music in his own right. Felix was the grandson of Moses Mendelssohn, the Jewish philosopher and founder of Reform Judaism, but Felix's father had his son baptized in the Lutheran Church in Berlin at the age of eight. This "conversion" may have had social advancement in mind (Felix's father was a banker), but Felix made significant contributions to both sacred music and church music (music for worship). As music director in Leipzig, Mendelssohn studied the Bach scores and led many concerts of Bach's major sacred works. Mendelssohn himself contributed several unaccompanied motets and nine settings of psalms to the church music repertoire. He also began a tradition in which people listen to the music of J. S. Bach, including his church music, in concert halls as well as churches—now even in non-Christian countries such as Japan, where Bach is very popular. "Old Bach," as he was called by King Frederick the Great, and whom Albert Schweitzer called "the fifth evangelist," may be Lutheranism's stealth witness to society.

Lutheran musicians have contributed significantly to church music in the United States. One may think of the celebrated college choirs of the Midwest or reputable composers of music for congregation, choir, and organ such as Jan Bender, Paul Bunjes, David Cherwien, Richard Hillert, Paul Manz and Carl Schalk. These musicians have drawn on the Lutheran tradition without being stuck in it. They have used the styles available today to accomplish their musical purposes, just as Bach put more "dance" into his music once he discovered Vivaldi.

The Cultural Content of Lutheran Identity

I have purposely ended with a discussion of the Lutheran contribution to the arts because Lutheran identity is bound up with a culture as well as a theological system, and the arts give expression to a culture.

To be sure, the Lutheran culture or way of life is informed by the Bible, confessions of faith, symbolical writings, liturgical practices, and hands-on work in society that aims to improve the quality of human life created in the image of God. This church culture can inform secular culture or stand athwart it, as opportunities and challenges require. We cannot abstract this church culture from the specific northern European ethnic heritages that received, contributed to, and passed on this culture. Neither are we bound to these ethnic heritages, as we see from the inculturation of Lutheranism in many "new worlds" in North and South America, east and southern Africa, southeast Asia, and Australia.[15] The content of Lutheranism transcends particular cultures, but Lutheranism is also a cultural reality that forms its adherents in the gospel of Christ.

Questions for Discussion

1. How did the Reformation contribute to social renewal?

2. What contributions did the Reformation make to the institution of marriage? How might the Reformation view of sex, marriage, and family contribute to contemporary understandings?

3. How did Lutherans address social needs through charitable institutions? What Lutheran social agencies serve the wider ministries of your congregation?

4. How do art and music contribute to the enrichment of society? How can congregations today be patrons of the arts?

Notes

Chapter 1

1. Heiko A. Oberman, *Luther: Man between God and the Devil*, trans. Eileen Walliser-Schwarzbart (New York: Doubleday Image, 1992), 50ff.

2. Ibid., 13ff.

3. See William Maltby, *The Reign of Charles V* (New York: Palgrave, 2002).

4. Martin Luther, "Ninety-Five Theses or Disputation on the Power and Efficacy of Indulgences," in *Luther's Works*, ed. Harold J. Grimm (Philadelphia: Fortress Press, 1957), 31:25, 28, 29.

5. Martin Luther, cited in Scott H. Hendrix, *Luther and the Papacy: Stages in a Reformation Conflict* (Philadelphia: Fortress Press, 1981), 83.

6. Edward Muir, *Ritual in Early Modern Europe*, New Approaches to European History (Cambridge: Cambridge University Press, 1997), 52. See also Frank C. Senn, *The People's Work: A Social History of the Liturgy* (Minneapolis: Fortress Press, 2006), ch. 12, "Death Here and Life Hereafter in the Middle Ages and the Reformation."

7. Martin Luther, "The Smalcald Articles," in *The Book of Concord*, ed. and trans. Theodore G. Tappert (Philadelphia: Fortress Press, 1959), 295.

8. Vilhelm Moberg, *A History of the Swedish People: From Renaissance to Revolution*, trans. Paul Britten Austin (New York: Pantheon, 1973), 169, writes, "So Sweden officially became an Evangelical Lutheran kingdom, with its own state Church, but a great deal of time was to pass before people were transformed spiritually from Catholics to Protestants. Here was no question of a spontaneous conversion; and it is quite possible that, but for Gustav Vasa's monetary straits, the Swedes would have remained Catholic to this day."

9. See Arthur Vööbus, *Studies in the History of the Estonian People* (Stockholm: Estonian Theological Society in Exile, 1970), 2:35–78.

10. Martin Luther, "On the Papacy in Rome against the Most Celebrated Romanist in Leipzig," in *Luther's Works*, ed. Eric W. Gritsch (Philadelphia: Fortress Press, 1970), 39:75.

11. Robert Kolb and Timothy J. Wengert, eds., *The Book of Concord* (Minneapolis: Fortress Press, 2000), 42.

12. Martin Luther, "On the Councils and the Church," in *Luther's Works*, ed. Eric W. Gritsch (Philadelphia: Fortress Press, 1966), 41:148–68.

Chapter 2

1. "Formula of Concord," Epitome, Article 1: "Original Sin," in *The Book of Concord*, ed. Theodore G. Tappert (Philadelphia: Fortress, 1959), 464.

2. For a fuller discussion, see Frank C. Senn, "The Bible and the Liturgy," *Liturgy: The Liturgy's Texts* 19, no. 3 (2004): 5–12.

3. For a discussion of the typological method and christological interpretation of the Old Testament, see Horace D. Hummel, *The Word Becoming Flesh: An Introduction to the Origin, Purpose, and Meaning of the Old Testament* (St. Louis: Concordia, 1979).

4. Martin Luther, "Confession Concerning Christ's Supper," in *Luther's Works*, ed. Robert H. Fischer (Philadelphia: Fortress Press, 1961), 37:254.

5. Brevard S. Childs, *Biblical Theology of the Old and New Testaments* (Minneapolis: Fortress Press, 1993).

6. Joseph Ratzinger (Pope Benedict XVI), *Jesus of Nazareth: From the Baptism in the Jordan to the Transfiguration*, trans. Adrian J. Walker (New York: Doubleday, 2007), xx.

Chapter 3

1. J. N. D. Kelly, *Early Christian Creeds*, 3rd ed. (London: Longmans, 1972), 211–30.

2. Martin Luther, *Luther's Werke: Kritische Gesamtausgabe* (Weimar: Herman Böhlaus Nachfolger, 1883ff.), 50:263, 6–11.

3. Josef A. Jungmann, *The Place of Christ in Liturgical Prayer*, trans. Geoffrey Chapman (Collegeville: Liturgical, 1965), 172–90.

4. Geoffrey Wainwright, *Doxology: The Praise of God in Worship, Doctrine, and Life* (New York: Oxford University Press, 1980), 186ff.

Chapter 4

1. "The Augsburg Confession," in *The Book of Concord*, ed. Theodore G. Tappert (Philadelphia: Fortress Press, 1959), 47.

2. Ibid., 95.

3. "The Augsburg Confession," Preface, in *The Book of Concord*, ed. Theodore G. Tappert (Philadelphia: Fortress Press, 1959), 26:13.

4. Eric W. Gritsch and Robert E. Jenson, in *Lutheranism: The Theological Movement and Its Confessional Writings* (Philadelphia: Fortress Press, 1978), develop the view that the article on justification by faith was a proposal of dogma for the Catholic Church.

5. Jaroslav Pelikan, *Obedient Rebels: Catholic Substance and Protestant Principle in Luther's Reformation* (New York: Harper & Row, 1964), 47–48.

6. C. F. W. Walther, *The Proper Distinction between Law and Gospel: Thirty-Nine Evening Lectures*, trans. W. H. T. Dau (St. Louis: Concordia, 1928), thesis II, 1:30.

7. Martin Luther, "The Small Catechism," in *The Book of Concord*, ed. Theodore G. Tappert (Philadelphia: Fortress Press, 1959), 338.

8. Martin Luther, "The Large Catechism," in *The Book of Concord*, ed. Theodore G. Tappert (Philadelphia: Fortress Press, 1959), 359.

9. See Steven Ozment, *Protestants: The Birth of a Revolution* (New York: Doubleday, 1992), 105–117.

10. "The Large Catechism," 437.

11. Martin Luther, "The Small Catechism (1529)," in *The Book of Concord: The Confessions of the Evangelical Lutheran Church*, ed. Robert Kolb and Timothy J. Wengert (Minneapolis: Fortress Press, 2000), 360.

12. "The Large Catechism," 466.

13. The text of the "Barmen Declaration" is easily accessed on the internet.

14. Carl E. Braaten, *Principles of Lutheran Theology* (Philadelphia: Fortress Press, 1983), 29–32.

15. The text of the "Joint Declaration on the Doctrine of Justification" is easily accessed on the internet.

Chapter 5

1. This includes the "short masses" (*missae brevis*) composed by Johann Sebastian Bach (1685–1750) for use in Leipzig. These short masses include only the Kyrie and Gloria. This was also the case with the great Mass in B Minor. The Kyrie and Gloria were composed in 1733 for a specific use in the electoral court at Dresden. But in 1749, when Bach completed the mass, he also drew upon a Sanctus that had been used in Leipzig in 1724. See Christoph Wolff, *Johann Sebastian Bach: The Learned Musician* (New York: Norton, 2000), 435ff.

2. The details of Muhlenberg's liturgy are found, in part, in *Documentary History of the Evangelical Lutheran Ministerium of Pennsylvania and Adjacent States: Proceedings of the Annual Conventions from 1748 to 1821* (Philadelphia: Board of Publications of the General Council of the Evangelical Lutheran Church in North America, 1898), 13–18. See also Beale M. Schmucker, "The First Pennsylvania Liturgy," *Lutheran Church Review* 1 (1882): 16–27, 161–172.

3. Actually, congregations received the ministerium's service with only the complaint that "The public service lasts too long." Pastors promised "to strive after brevity." *Documentary History*, 11.

4. Luther D. Reed, *The Lutheran Liturgy*, rev. ed. (Philadelphia: Fortress Press, 1959), 164ff.

5. On the primacy of prayer (the experience of God) over belief (reflection about God) see Aidan Kavanagh, *On Liturgical Theology* (New York: Pueblo, 1984), 91ff.

6. "Apology of the Augsburg Confession," in *The Book of Concord*, ed. Theodore G. Tappert (Philadelphia: Fortress Press, 1959), 230.

7. "The Small Catechism," in *The Book of Concord*, ed. Theodore G. Tappert (Philadelphia: Fortress Press, 1959), 347.

Chapter 6

1. Carter Lindberg, *Beyond Charity: Reformation Initiatives for the Poor* (Minneapolis: Fortress Press, 1993).

2. See Eamon Duffy, *The Stripping of the Altar: Traditional Religion in England 1400–1580* (New Haven: Yale University Press, 1992), 355ff, 504ff.

3. Martin Luther, "The Christian in Society," in *Luther's Works*, American Ed., (Philadephia: Fortress Press, 1962), 45:392.

4. Steven Ozment, *Protestants: The Birth of a Revolution* (New York: Doubleday, 1992), 163.

5. Martin Luther, "A Marriage Booklet for Simple Pastors," in *The Book of Concord*, ed. Robert Kolb and Timothy J. Wengert (Minneapolis: Fortress Press, 2000), 367–71. See also Frank C. Senn, *The People's Work: A Social History of the Liturgy* (Minneapolis: Fortress Press, 2006), ch. 13, "The Ecclesiastical Captivity of Marriage."

6. See Philip Jacob Spener, *Pia Desideria*, trans. and ed. Theodore G. Tappert (Philadelphia: Fortress Press, 1964).

7. See Eric W. Gritsch, *A History of Lutheranism* (Minneapolis: Fortress Press, 2002), 146–50.

8. See *ibid.*, 184–89, on these and other examples of inner mission work.

9. Martin Luther, "Third Lenten Sermon (11 March 1522)," in *Luther's Works*, American Ed., 51 (Philadelphia: Muhlenberg, 1959), 82–83.

10. See Bodo Nischan, *Prince, People, and Confession: The Second Reformation in Brandenburg* (Philadelphia: University of Pennsylvania Press, 1994), 146.

11. Carl Christensen, *Art and Reformation in Germany* (Athens: Ohio University Press, 1979), 151.

12. See Joseph Herl, *Worship Wars in Early Lutheranism: Choir, Congregation, and Three Centuries of Conflict* (Oxford: Oxford University Press, 2004).

13. Friedrich Blume, ed., *Protestant Church Music* (New York: Norton, 1974), 122.

14. See the data for popular Lutheran resistance to a Calvinist regime amassed by Bodo Nischan, *op. cit.*, 161ff.

15. See the Lutheran World Federation studies on "Worship and Culture," especially *Worship and Culture in Dialogue*. Reports of International Consultations in Cartigny, Switzerland, 1993 and Hong Kong, 1994, ed. S. Anita Stauffer (Geneva: Lutheran World Federation, 1994).

For Further Reading

Chapter 1

Bainton, Roland. *Here I Stand: A Life of Martin Luther*. New York: Abingdon-Cokesbury, 1950.

Gritsch, Eric W. *Fortress Introduction to Lutheranism*. Minneapolis: Fortress Press, 1994.

————. *A History of Lutheranism*. Minneapolis: Fortress Press, 2002.

Lathrop, Gordon W., and Timothy J. Wengert. *Christian Assembly: Marks of the Church in a Pluralistic Age*. Minneapolis: Fortress Press, 2004.

Luther, Martin. *Three Treatises*. From the American Edition of *Luther's Works*. Minneapolis: Fortress Press, 1947.

Marty, Martin. *Martin Luther*. New York: Penguin, 2004.

Nelson, E. Clifford, ed. *The Lutherans in North America*. Minneapolis: Fortress Press, 1975.

Nestingen, James A. *Martin Luther: A Life*. Minneapolis: Augsburg Books, 2003.

Chapter 2

Braaten, Carl E., and Robert W. Jenson, eds. *Reclaiming the Bible for the Church*. Grand Rapids, Mich.: Eerdmans, 1995.

Pelikan, Jaroslav. *Whose Bible Is It? A History of the Scriptures through the Ages*. New York: Viking Penguin, 2005.

Chapter 3

Kelly, J. N. D. *Early Christian Creeds*, 3rd ed. London: Longmans, 1972.

Pelikan, Jaroslav. *Credo: Historical and Theological Guide to the Creeds and Confessions of Faith of the Christian Tradition*. New Haven, Conn.: Yale University Press, 2005.

Chapter 4

Allbeck, Willard D. *Studies in the Lutheran Confessions*, rev. ed. Philadelphia: Fortress Press, 1968.

Braaten, Carl E. *Principles of Lutheran Theology*, rev. ed. Minneapolis: Fortress Press, 2007. See chapter 2, "The Confessional Principle."

Gassmann, Günther, and Scott Hendrix. *Fortress Introduction to the Lutheran Confessions*. Minneapolis: Fortress Press, 1999.

Gritsch, Eric W., and Robert W. Jenson. *Lutheranism: The Theological Movement and Its Confessional Writings*. Philadelphia: Fortress Press, 1976.

Kohl, Robert, and Timothy Wengert, trans. and ed. *The Book of Concord*. Minneapolis: Fortress Press, 2000.

Tappert, Theodore G., trans. and ed. *The Book of Concord*. In collaboration with Jaroslav Pelikan, Robert H. Fischer, and Arthur C. Piepkorn. Philadelphia: Fortress Press, 1959.

Chapter 5

Pfatteicher, Phillip H. *Commentary on the Lutheran Book of Worship*. Minneapolis: Augsburg Fortress, 1990.

———. *Commentary on the Occasional Services*. Philadelphia: Fortress Press, 1983.

Reed, Luther D. *The Lutheran Liturgy*, rev. ed. Philadelphia: Fortress Press, 1959.

Senn, Frank C. *Christian Liturgy—Catholic and Evangelical*. Minneapolis: Fortress Press, 1997. See especially parts 2 and 3.

———. *The People's Work: A Social History of the Liturgy* (Minneapolis: Fortress Press, 2006. See especially chs. 10, 11, 14, and 15.

———. *Protestant Spiritual Traditions*. Mahwah, N.J.: Paulist, 1986. Reprinted by Wipf and Stock, Eugene, Ore. See especially ch. 1, "Lutheran Spirituality."

Chapter 6

Lazareth, William H. *Christians in Society: Luther, the Bible, and Social Ethics*. Minneapolis: Fortress Press, 2001.

Lindberg, Carter. *Beyond Charity: Reformation Initiatives for the Poor*. Minneapolis: Fortress Press, 1993.

Ozment, Steven. *Protestants: The Birth of a Revolution*. New York: Doubleday, 1992.

Pelikan, Jaroslav. *Bach among the Theologians*. Philadelphia: Fortress Press, 1983.

Weborg, John. "Pietism: 'The Fire of God Which . . . Flames in the Heart of Germany.'" In *Protestant Spiritual Traditions*, ed. Frank C. Senn, 183–216. Mahwah, N.J.: Paulist, 1986. Reprinted by Wipf & Stock, Eugene, Ore.